THE
MEMORIAL
HOSPITAL SYSTEM:
THE FIRST SEVENTY-FIVE YEARS

The
Memorial
Hospital System:
The First Seventy-Five Years

*Commemorating the
75th Anniversary of
The Memorial Hospital
System, 1907—1982*

*TED FRANCIS
AND
CAROLE McFARLAND*

LARKSDALE

HOUSTON

THE MEMORIAL HOSPITAL SYSTEM:

THE FIRST SEVENTY-FIVE YEARS

Copyright 1982 by Memorial Hospital System

Commemorative Edition, November 1982

ISBN 0-89896-074-6

Editing and Book Design, Frances L. Burke
Cover Art, Douglas James
Index Design, Margaret Bartlett

LARKSDALE

HOUSTON

Printed in the United States of America

FOREWORD

THE celebration of the Memorial Hospital System's 75th year affords an appropriate time for all its employees and friends to reflect on the history of this great institution. Too often, the pressures of providing health care on a day-to-day basis mean that we do not have, or do not take, the time to look at our past. We need to know not only the larger tradition of hospital development, but also our own institution's history and its place in that larger development.

Memorial has survived and flourished partly because its timing and location were right. The main element in its success, however, has been the dedication over the years of its administrators, trustees, medical staff, and employees. When I proposed to celebrate Memorial's 75th birthday with a written history, I wanted such a history to offer each of us connected with the hospital a convenient way to become reacquainted with the loyalty and the dedication of those who have helped build this hospital. I also hoped that such a history would be entertaining.

Memorial has a lively and spirited past as well as an impressive present, and I hope that the narrative ranging from 1907 to 1982 will convey some of that vitality. I have read the manuscript for *The Memorial Hospital System: The First Seventy-Five Years*, and I believe it celebrates the hospital's birthday with a chronicle which catches the major events and people of these 75 years, as well as the spirit of the institution. My hope is that you will read it with pleasure.

W. WILSON TURNER
AUGUST 1982

PREFACE

Houston's Memorial Hospital System has always been closely tied to the city it serves. When the hospital first came into being at the turn of the century, the city was still relatively new and small. Houston, by one count made at that time, had only one other hospital, 12 public schools, and a shell road running as far as Harrisburg. What is now Memorial Drive was then only a dirt road.

The institution which has become the Memorial Hospital System was also small. The first home for the hospital, purchased in 1907, was a wooden building with room for only 17 beds. It had a laboratory equipped with one microscope, ten test tubes, and an alcohol burner. The Baptist Sanitarium, as it was first called, was staffed with eight trained nurses who cooked patient meals, cleaned rooms, mixed and gave medications, bathed patients, gave nightly back rubs and kept records. The first administrator for the hospital, the Reverend D. R. Pevoto, wrote: "In those days a hospital was looked upon with apprehension as just a place where people went to die. We decided to change all that."

Reverend Pevoto was right. American attitudes toward health care and hospitals have changed; he was right, too, to claim that the hospital he founded would play an important role in such change. That spirit of innovation which he voiced has led the institution through 75 years of growth.

The hospital had the first chartered school of nursing in Houston, and it was the first general hospital in the city to add psychiatric care. Memorial also received the state's first shipment of the then new "wonder drug," penicillin, in 1943. It was a national pioneer in the move toward hospital satellite systems, the plan whereby smaller satellite hospitals, backed always by the specialized facilities, equipment, and personnel of the central unit, take their hospital beds and services to the expanding suburban areas of the city.

Even Reverend Pevoto, however, would be amazed at the size of the institution which has grown from that first frame building. The hospital, like the city, has never stopped growing. The once tiny hospital, located on a piece of land 40 by 75 feet, now occupies about 1 million square feet of floor space. It is a total health care system with over 3,500 employees and more than 1,000 hospital beds. The system includes the new major medical complex in southwest Houston, plus an administrative services building, also in the southwest, and satellite hospitals in the southeast and northwest quadrants of the city. It also has affiliations with other hospitals in the area which are either leased or managed. It conducts a number of medical education programs including schools of X-ray technology, medical technology and inhalation therapy, medical residencies, administrative residencies, clinical pastoral education, and a program for licensed vocational nursing. It also provides clinical facilities for a baccalaureate program in nursing and a master's program in speech pathology.

The first 75 years of innovation and growth have, however, left one crucial aspect of the hospital unchanged: its tradition of caring. Any history of the Memorial Hospital System is really a chronicle of the care expressed over the years by the administrators, medical staff, and employees of the Memorial Hospital System. Their concern for the people of Houston, and their dedication to providing truly excellent medical care for them, prompts this history of *The Memorial Hospital System: The First Seventy-Five Years.*

ACKNOWLEDGMENTS

A commemorative history such as this one, written to honor Memorial Hospital's 75th anniversary, can never be the work of any one or two people. Since we started work on the book in October 1981, a number of people have helped us in various parts of its preparation. Many of the people who figure prominently in the events described in the book were interviewed, and, without exception, the interviewees were helpful and willing to share their memories with us.

Although this is a limited history, we did consult a variety of materials on the history of Memorial Hospital. Among those who helped us find early documents about the hospital, we want to give special thanks to Mrs. Elizabeth White, the Curator for Special Collections at the Houston Academy of Medicine in the Texas Medical Center. She went out of her way to open the collection there for our use on nights and weekends. Equally helpful were two members of Memorial's staff: Mr. James Landureth, Audio-Visual Director, who opened his files to us and helped us search for the specific photographs we needed, and Mr. Michael Halloway of the Photography Department, who also shared his files with us and graciously took many photographs of old records and newspapers for use in this book.

The materials provided by such hospital publications as *The Satellite, Scope,* and *Caring* have also been important sources of information about the hospital. For information about the city of Houston, we relied heavily on David G. McComb's thorough *Houston: A History.* Much of the information on the city comes from his book.

Special gratitude is due two people whose help and encouragement were instrumental in preparing the book. Mr. Marco Milazzo, Director of Public Relations for the Memorial Hospital System, freely shared all of the information available to him and guided us to many sources of material. Equally useful were his enthusiasm for this project and his knowledge of the hospital's history. Finally, we want to acknowledge a special debt to Mr. W. Wilson Turner, longtime Chief Administrator of the hospital and now President Emeritus of the System. His knowledge of the hospital is, of course, extensive and his help in setting up interviews and locating information was invaluable. He feels deeply involved with the hospital and its history; we are grateful for his guidance throughout the project.

We want to say a final word about the scope and the design of this history. We do not intend for it to be a comprehensive, scholarly account of Houston health care, or of the Memorial Hospital System. We do want it to be an interesting, reasonably lively, and readable narrative. It is designed both to preserve some of the key events and personalities of Memorial's past and to help the hospital celebrate its 75th year.

August, 1982
Ted Francis
Carole McFarland

LIST OF INTERVIEWS

Mr. B. J. Bradshaw

Miss Marie Burgin

Chaplain Tom Cole

Mrs. Fred Couper

Mrs. Mary DeFoy

Mrs. John Dudley

Mr. L. E. Frazier, Jr.

Mr. Vernon G. Garrett, Jr.

Miss Jeanette James

Chaplain Joe Fred Luck

Dr. B. J. Martin

Mr. Marco Milazzo

Mr. Kenneth E. Montague

Mr. John Orr

Mr. W. Wilson Turner

Mrs. Ruth Walker

Mr. and Mrs. Fred Walters

Mr. R. William Warren

CONTENTS

**The
Memorial
Hospital System:**
The First Seventy-Five Years

CHAPTER ONE

The Committee deems it proper to say, for the information of the Convention, that this Sanitarium has been in operation about three years; that it has already accomplished much good; that its location is most advantageous for such an enterprise; that it is now more than paying its way, and that it is constantly growing in public favor, not only in the great commercial center where it is located, but also in the regions round about.

THE EARLY YEARS   1907 - 1924

THE BIRTH OF A HOSPITAL: 1907 - 1910

The discussion which gave birth to the Memorial Hospital System can best be described in the words of a man who was there. The Reverend D. R. Pevoto, then pastor of the Clark Avenue Baptist Church, provides this account of the talk held during a revival meeting in 1904:

> *Just before leaving Clark Street Church, Dr. L. T. Mays, founder and first pastor of Tuam Avenue Baptist Church (now South Main) assisted me in a meeting. We were housed in one day by a cold rain. As we sat he said, "We need a hospital, a real religious institution." It was a proposition. We selected some Baptist doctors and conferred with them. The verdict was the same. "We certainly need more and better hospital accommodations, but . . ."*

Rev. Pevoto took three years to turn that proposition into an actual hospital. The years were filled with interviews (one was with Mr. George Hermann who liked the idea of a hospital but did not want a religious institution) in which he found many people who wanted a hospital. No one, however, wanted the responsibility for it.

Two things finally happened which made it possible for Rev. Pevoto himself to pursue the project. One was that the Rudisill Sanitarium, located at the corner of Smith and Lamar at the end of the trolley line, came up for sale. The key change, however, came in 1907 when Rev. Pevoto was offered the position of assistant pastor at the First Baptist Church. Since he had already decided that he needed support from that church if anything was to come of his hospital efforts, he took the job. He found the pastor of the church, Dr. J. L. Gross, at first reluctant to consider the scheme. He kept talking, however, until he interested some members of the church and until he finally converted Dr. Gross to the idea.

Even then there was one last obstacle, one which took a form familiar to those who know the rivalry between Texas' two largest cities. Rev. Pevoto relates that they were just ready to launch their institution when the Texas Baptist General Convention discussed a plan to build a statewide Baptist hospital in Dallas. Rev. Pevoto's group backed off, waited a while, and then decided, as any good Houstonian would have, that "a hospital in Dallas would not help Houston."

Thus it was that in August of 1907 a Board of Trustees was elected, a charter procured, and the Rudisill Sanitarium purchased and renamed the Baptist Sanitarium. The two-story frame and brick-veneer building was bought for $18,000. Rev. Pevoto relates that: "We paid all cash except $17,000." Those were depression years, and the $1,000 cash which made the purchase possible was given by a church member, Mrs. Charles Stewart. The Sanitarium came under Baptist control on September 1, 1907. Dr. Gross, by now an enthusiastic backer, served as President of the Board of Trustees, and Rev. Pevoto was Board Secretary-Treasurer and Hospital General Manager. Mrs. Ida J. Rudisill was appointed Superintendent of Nurses.

Rev. Pevoto, as he candidly admitted, had entered a new field; he "knew absolutely nothing about a hospital." We must assume that Rev. Pevoto learned quickly, however, because he soon was elected Superintendent, a post he held until December 1917. During those ten years, he visited and studied hospitals throughout the East and North. The visits taught him much more about hospitals, and the more he learned, the more convinced he became that this project was different, that there were "no institutions of its exact kind with which to compare it." He reports that this was the second hospital under Baptist control and management; the first one, the Missouri Baptist Sanitarium, offered no useful model because it was in the older city of St. Louis.

His pioneer hospital in a pioneer city offered a number of challenges, but the chief one was simply the difficulty of keeping enough hospital space for the city's growing

18

population. Despite the additions during his years, Rev. Pevoto's constant regret was "insufficient room and no money for enlargement." This pioneer status, however, also had its advantages. Rev. Pevoto cheerfully notes, for example, that his "work, though imperfect, was practically free from invidious comparisons."

The new hospital also provided a more serious advantage: the chance to introduce new ways of doing things. Of the two innovations which gave him most pride, one was in nursing education. He relates that each of the student nurses had a course in Bible. When the nurse left the sanitarium training school, she took with her two diplomas—one the standard nursing diploma and the other a Sunday School Teacher's Diploma issued by the Baptist Sunday School Board in Nashville. Rev. Pevoto also speaks with pride of another change, one which enabled the hospital to treat patients without distinctions based on class or financial condition. Since there was no separate charity ward and since even the nurses did not know which patients were admitted free, the hospital could do charity work without branding any patient a "charity case."

This first period ends with a special meeting of the Board of Directors held on November 9, 1910. T. M. Kennerly, Board Secretary, offered a resolution that the hospital be affiliated with the Baptist General Convention of Texas. This resolution was adopted unanimously by the Board, and it was then sent on to the Convention and a special 10-member committee. They accepted, of course, and the terms of that acceptance summarize the hospital's first three years:

> *The Committee deems it proper to say, for the information of the Convention, that this Sanitarium has been in operation about three years; that it has already accomplished much good; that its location is most advantageous for such an enterprise; that it is now more than paying its way, and that it is constantly growing in public favor, not only in the great commercial center where it is located, but also in the regions round about.*

19

The Original Baptist Sanitarium, Formerly
the Rudisill Sanitarium. (Note the Hitching
Posts in Front)

THE BAPTIST SANITARIUM OFFICE

A SIDE VIEW OF THE ORIGINAL BUILDING IN 1908

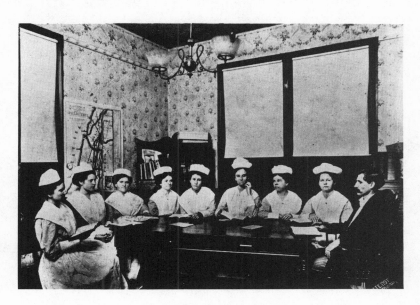

Rev. Pevoto Teaching Bible Study to the
First Nursing School Class

BAPTIST SANITARIUM
OF HOUSTON, TEXAS

PHONE 1374   602 LAMAR AVENUE

A STRICTLY FIRST-CLASS INSTITUTION, WITH ALL HOME
COMFORTS. AN ENTIRELY NEW BUILDING WITH ALL THE
MODERN IMPROVEMENTS. TRAINED NURSES IN ATTENDANCE.

RATES: FROM TWO TO FIVE DOLLARS PER DAY

MRS. IDA J. RUDISILL   .   .   SUPERINTENDENT
D. R. PEVOTO, CORRESPONDING SECRETARY-TREASURER

Dr. P.G. Sears,   HOUSTON. TEXAS, Jany. 4th 1908.
1117 Tex. Ave, Houston, Tex.

    Dear Brother:-

        The inclosed circular contains words of
equal interest to all; especially that part which tells of "Service
Rendered" and "Aims and Necessities". We are position to assist you
in the charity work you wish your church to do by meeting you half
way in the expenses of such work. That is to say, we will give you
our regular $2.00 per day service for $1.00; i.e. for $365., a private room
will be kept exclusively for your work for one year, or 365 days of
service will be given for $365.; provided the service be taken in 12
months. This includes free ambulance service, operating room, regular
nursing, and medicine, except prescriptions, wines or mineral waters.

    It does not include special nurse, nor personal laundry.
Should a private room for $365. a year straight time be chosen and she
should be vacant at any time that we can use at at the regular rate of
$2.00 per day, $1.00 will be given to you; or the room will be held
subject to your orders. If you are interested in this plan and we can
be of service to you, I would be glad to talk over the matter more
fully with you.   For the present I beg to remain,

              Yours fraternally,

           D R Pevoto . Cor. Secy, & Treas.

Charter

THE STATE OF TEXAS,
COUNTY OF HARRIS.

Know All Men by These Presents—

That we, T. M. Kennerly, J. L. Gross and Robert Carroll, of Houston, Harris County, Texas, together with the other persons hereinafter mentioned, and together with various and other citizens of the State of Texas, by these presents do associate ourselves together and form a body corporate under and by virtue of the laws of Texas, and do hereby agree upon the following charter:

ARTICLE I.

The name of this corporation shall be BAPTIST SANITARIUM AND HOSPITAL.

ARTICLE II.

The purposes for which this corporation is formed are purely benevolent, charitable, educational and religious, and not for financial gain, and no financial gain shall ever accrue to any member of this corporation, or any other person or institution in the conduct of same, but any receipts of this corporation in excess of the expense of purchase, or erection and maintenance of the said institution provided for herein, shall be applied by the Directors to the care of charity patients, and to the equipment and enlargement of said institutions, to carry out the purposes of its organization and operation, as they in their judgment may deem wise. It is organized to acquire or erect, and to equip, conduct and maintain on the broadest humanitarian principles, a hospital or hospitals, and training school or schools for nurses, to care for the sick and injured, and to educate and train persons in the care of the sick and injured, issuing to such persons diplomas upon graduation, and erecting and conducting such hospital or hospitals, school or schools, or other institutions as may be necessary or desirable to carry out all of said purposes, to the end, also, that the souls of men may be healed. Said institutions shall be open alike to all legal and reputable physicians and surgeons, and to all reputable medical schools. All patients shall be at liberty to choose their own spiritual advisers, and such advisers shall be received with every courtesy, and religious liberty shall be preserved alike to all, and no religious test whatever shall be made.

ARTICLE III.

The principal office and place of business of this corporation shall be in the City of Houston, Harris County, Texas, at which place its business shall be transacted.

ARTICLE IV.

This corporation shall exist for a period of fifty (50) years.

ARTICLE V.

This corporation shall have fifteen (15) Directors, to be elected by the Baptist General Convention of Texas, each of whom must be a member of a Baptist church, and a resident of the State of Texas, and no physician shall be elibible to membership on said Board. The Board of Directors for the first year shall be as follows:

Class A—

    J. L. Gross, of Houston, Harris County, Texas;
    F. L. Berry, of Houston, Harris County, Texas;
    Robert Carroll, of Houston, Harris County, Texas;
    R. E. Burt, of Houston, Harris County, Texas;
    M. E. Weaver, of Bryan, Brazos County, Texas.

Class B—

    T. M. Kennerly, of Houston, Harris County, Texas;
    W. C. Munn, of Houston, Harris County, Texas;
    J. W. Neal, of Houston, Harris County, Texas;
    N. P. Teague, of Rosenberg, Fort Bend County, Texas;
    W. R. Stockwell, of Alvin, Brazoria County, Texas.

The affiliation with the Convention brought with it additions to the hospital and a name change from Baptist Sanitarium to the Baptist Sanitarium and Hospital. The first of these additions, shown in the picture taken from the Superintendent's report of the year 1911, was a four-story addition to the rear of the building. This increased the hospital's capacity by 50 beds.

Dr. Gross remembered that "we thought that if we could have all beds occupied within two years, we would regard ourselves as very fortunate, indeed." Instead, within 60 days, the hospital was again full and turning away patients. Soon he notes that the hospital had turned away as many as 11 patients in one day and 32 in one week. The hospital clearly needed to expand again, but such enlargement came about only after a great deal of concern about financing. The hospital representatives first tried an unsuccessful fund-raising trip to the Baptist General Convention. Dr. Gross then tells us that "in answer to prayer, we believe, Mr. W. T. Carter agreed to give us $5,000 payable monthly, in case we could raise $50,000, and Deacon R. E. Burt, with the hearty concurrence of his family, gave us $10,000, payable as the work progressed without condition."

The next enlargement came in 1914, raising the four-story building to eight stories and increasing the capacity by 100 beds. But still the matters of size and money occupied most of the hospital administration's time. The Superintendent's reports always echoed the views expressed in his 1913 report:

> *Our prosperity in the matter of securing*
> *patients had become our greatest problem . . .*
> *we have not been able to take care of more than*
> *one third who have applied for treatment.*

These severe pressures did not, however, ever lead to a reduction in the quality of medical care. The same year the Board report makes this statement:

The report of our Superintendent shows that the average cost of maintenance per patient was $2.42 per day. This seems to be quite a large sum, but when we remember that our ideals demand that we shall render the very best possible service, we will recall that this cannot be done without a correspondingly large expense. Indeed, that institution which seeks to cut down the cost of maintenance at the expense of the best efficiency only advertises itself as a back number, and as being without the spirit of the highest form of altruism.

THE BABY CAMP AND ROOF GARDEN

Medical progress was also made during this period, and the hospital was no prouder of any service than of its baby camp. A women's group, named the Settlement Association of Houston, had for a number of years provided special infant care. The mortality among babies at this time was severe; for example, in the United States in 1908, 375,000 babies died. Experts estimated that some three-fourths of these could have been saved with proper care, and the Settlement had tried to provide such care for those sick babies whose parents could not take them out of the city's heat and noise. The hospital took on this health problem. With typical energy, they resolved to build:

. . . a thoroughly scientific and modern roof garden on top of the sixth story of the building, specially fitted up and equipped for a baby camp of sufficient capacity to care for 50 patients.

The enthusiasm for the project pictured below can be seen in the language which Dr. Gross uses to describe it:

Situated up here above the noise and dust, mosquitoes and flies, and thoroughly screened, treated after the most skillful method and nursed with sterilized, wholesome food, and having an abundance of God's fresh air and sunshine, it was believed that many of the children who otherwise would succumb to the summer's heat, could be saved and sent out into the world as healthy, vigourous children.

Another point of pride for the hospital was the Maternity Department which occupied an entire floor. Dr. Gross tells us that this institution was becoming "deservedly popular." Even though there was dust and noise from the building construction, 1913 saw that "57 happy mothers passed through this dark, dangerous valley and have come out to the sunny hills on the other side, happy, comfortable, and safe, and with a new life breathing in their arms."

Still another outstanding feature of the institution was the nursing school. Founded along with the hospital in 1907 and named the Baptist Sanitarium Training School for Graduate Nurses, it was now "doing a very high grade of work in training a large number of young women for this noble service." This, the first chartered school of nursing in Houston, began with a two-year course of study and graduated its first class of seven nurses in 1909. In 1910, the school changed its name to the Baptist Sanitarium and Hospital Training School, and in 1914, the course length was extended to three years. Soon afterward, the school attained Miss Retta Johnson, its first full-time instructor and one of only ten in the United States. She worked at the hospital from 1916 until 1926 and was prominent in professional affairs, serving as a charter member of the local Nurse's Association.

It was also at this time, soon after the beginning of the nursing school, that an event occurred which would shape the history of the school for many years to come. In 1908, Miss Lillian Wilson—later to become Mrs. Robert Jolly—came to work at the school from Louisville, Kentucky, where she had graduated from the School of Nursing at the Kentucky School of Medicine. Her official duties put her in charge of the operating room, but, according to Reverend Pevoto's account, her actual responsibilities were much broader. Miss Wilson was on duty 24 hours a day, being on call at all hours of the night in Surgery, Obstetrics and every department. Mrs. Rudisill, who had wanted to resign for several years, resigned sometime during the end of 1911 or the first of 1912, and Miss Wilson took on the title of Nursing Director. She soon gave indication of the high educational standards which would characterize her more than 40 years of service by hiring two full-time instructors of nursing.

Another important staff member was Mrs. George Lee, employed by the hospital as its Missionary to work with patients, nurses, and other employees in the Institution. The hospital emphasized that "this religious work is pursued only among those patients willing to receive same and is pressed upon no one not willing to receive it." Yet no opportunity was "overlooked to win the lost, or to reclaim those who have gone astray." The hospital's yearly report for 1912 showed:

Bedside visits 4835
Service in wards 130
Letters written 275
Conversions 85
Backsliders reclaimed 97
Devotional services for nurses 552
Bible classes for nurses 54

Soon after this first rapid period of growth, the hospital underwent its first change of administration. Rev. Pevoto resigned on December 31, 1917, to become Assistant Secretary of the Executive Board of the Baptist General Convention, and was replaced temporarily by the Director of Nurses, Mrs. J. P. Burnett, the former Lillian Wilson. She filled the position until January 1, 1919, when the hospital entered a new, long-term period of administrative stability by hiring Mr. Robert Jolly as Business Manager. Mr. Jolly, who became Superintendent on January 1, 1920, had come to Houston from Kentucky as Assistant to the Pastor of the First Baptist Church. He had been working at First Baptist for slightly over a year and, while visiting patients, had become interested in the hospital's work. Thus, even before he began his 27 years as Superintendent, Mr. Jolly knew something of Memorial's problems and its potential.

THE SANITARIUM'S FIRST X-RAY MACHINE

It is not surprising, then, that one of his first acts was to secure an X-ray machine for the hospital. The absence of such a machine at the Baptist Sanitarium had made operations cumbersome in the extreme. If a patient needed an X-ray, he had to be brought down to the ambulance entrance, put in an ambulance, taken down to the Carter building at the corner of Main and Rusk, and then taken up the elevator to Dr. Van Zant's X-ray Department. It was obvious that the hospital needed an X-ray Department of its own, but the price was a formidable $6,000.

Undaunted, Mr. Jolly set out to raise the money. One of the men to whom he appealed for funds was the oil man, W. C. Turnbow. He did not want to give the hospital the whole $6,000, but Mr. Jolly did finally persuade him to give $1,000. Mr. Turnbow's money would be forthcoming, however, only after one crucial condition was met: the balance of the cost had to be raised. Mr. Jolly's quick response demonstrated the resourcefulness and energy characteristic of his leadership. He asked Mr. Turnbow to give him a check for $1,000 then and there, promising him that the check would not be cashed until the remainder was secured. Then he set out with a $1,000 check to use in soliciting money from others.

Mr. Jolly was much in demand as a song leader, and when the Eagle Lake Baptist Church asked him to lead the singing in a two-week revival meeting, he saw another opportunity to raise money. He agreed to lead the singing, but only if the church would contribute toward the hospital X-ray machine. Every day for two weeks, he would leave Houston on the afternoon train for Eagle Lake, lead the singing in the big tent meeting, spend the night at Eagle Lake, then rise at sun-up the next morning to catch the Houston train in time for his work at the hospital. The arduous schedule paid off. When the revival meeting ended, the Eagle Lake Baptist Church contributed $1,200 for the X-ray Department. After such hard work on his part, it must have been hard to turn Mr. Jolly down. He solicited funds from other churches and individuals for several months until he reached the goal, then showed the receipts to Mr. Turnbow, and cashed the $1,000 check. Baptist Sanitarium soon had its first X-ray Department.

HOSPITAL CERTIFICATION BY AMERICAN COLLEGE OF SURGEONS

The need for Mr. Jolly's skill did not stop with this first triumph. These early years of his administration were a time when the world of medicine changed rapidly. World War I brought advancement in surgical skills and anesthesiology, special training for operating room technicians and the emergence of radiology as a diagnostic tool. In 1918 the American College of Surgeons offered hospital certification to hospitals meeting its high standards. The Baptist Sanitarium was a strong supporter of this movement toward national standards for hospitals, but this did not mean approval was instant. In Texas, as in the rest of the United States, only a few hospitals were found eligible at first.

In 1921, Dr. Williamson, an Inspector for the American College of Surgeons, made his first visit to the Baptist Sanitarium. The first thing that he asked Mr. Jolly to show him was the Pathological Laboratory. Since the laboratory at that time was only a little room, eight by eight feet, with ten test tubes and one microscope, Mr. Jolly tried to distract his visitor by pointing out other features of the hospital. When Dr. Williamson insisted and was finally shown the laboratory, he told Mr. Jolly that: "You will have to get a real laboratory before the hospital can be approved." Mr. Jolly replied: "When you come back next time we will show you a laboratory that will be unsurpassed anywhere in Texas."

Dr. Williamson then asked to see the Medical Record

Librarian's Department. Again, Mr. Jolly tried unsuccessfully to divert his attention. Finally, he showed him the only records kept at the time: a list showing the patient's name and address, the name of his doctor, and the ambulance which had brought him to the hospital. Dr. Williamson's earlier statement was repeated and so was Mr. Jolly's answer. Next year the inspection ended differently. Dr. Williamson was again the inspector, but this time he admitted that he had never seen a better Laboratory or Record Librarian's Department. The hospital was placed on the approved list of the American College of Surgeons immediately and has remained there since that time.

It was also during this time that Mr. Jolly went to work on his project of publicizing the Obstetrical Department of Baptist Hospital. This was the first of two such efforts that he made, and it, like his subsequent material/price reduction during the depression, had a dual purpose. At the same time that he wanted to make sure his own maternity department was well known, Mr. Jolly also sought to provide the public with badly needed general medical education. This was a period when only a small percentage of the babies born in Houston were born in a hospital, and the public needed to be made aware that babies born in hospitals had a better chance of survival. Therefore, he scheduled on May 12, (Florence Nightingale's birthday), 1923, a giant party on the hospital lawn. Every child that had been born at the hospital was invited, and the crowds were so great that the police had to be called to control traffic.

Mr. Jolly still had to contend with the shortage of beds, which had been a problem for Rev. Pevoto, and he sought money to expand the hospital again. One early effort came in the statement made by him to the Board in October of 1920. The letter, which follows, shows both his formidable energy and his resolve to have the hospital enlarged. One result of this was a not-very-successful local campaign for funds; the other was his subsequent appeal to the General Convention.

BAPTIST SANITARIUM
HOUSTON, TEXAS

TO BOARD OF DIRECTORS OF BAPTIST SANITARIUM.

Gentlemen:-

This is not a report, but simply a statement of some of my work for ten months ending Oct. 8th-1920. I am making the statement that those of you who have not been in close touch with the institution may know whether I have been worth anything to the institution.

During that time I have traveled 12,900 Miles in the interest of the hospital and the denomination. Of course you know that when I spoke on any phase of denominational work I spoke on the sanitarium and got money for it everywhere I went. Whenever I was invited to a place to speak or sing for any sort of meeting, I made it a rule never to leave without a drive for the hospital and its funds.

In the ten months I made fifty three speeches for the denomination's 75 million Campaign and Loyalty Bonds, and fifty five for the hospital making a total of one hundred and eight speeches, and I did not keep account of solos sung. Happen to remember that in one place I sang fourteen solos in one day.

In the ten months I secured for linen etc.	*$4806.00*
For X-Ray Equipment	*5000.00*
For operating room equipment from M. E. Foster,	*800.00*
	$10,606.00

I never was happier in my life and if the members of the Board will make a sacrifice of their valuable time, and get at the building proposition right now, we will have a great hospital. We are actually losing ground and prestige in Houston today, for the Doctors and patients are being denied rooms daily and it has gotten on their nerves, and many of them are, as they express it, disgusted. Lets start something.

Robert Jolly

31

In the early twenties, Mr. Jolly requested money from the Executive Board of the Baptist General Convention. After a speech which outlined the needs of the hospital, he amazed everyone at the meeting by asking for the huge sum of $405,000. It took a great deal of persuasion, but the Board did include that amount as part of what was called the Seventy-five Million Campaign for Baptist institutions. The total goal was not reached, however, and the hospital received only about $83,000 of the original request. This money was put to use immediately when the Board of Trustees bought the remainder of the block (except for a cottage on the corner of Dallas and Smith purchased later) on which the hospital was located. A large 100-bed addition at the corner of Lamar and Smith was finally constructed in 1924. To build it, the hospital took out a loan of $300,000 and a second mortgage of $100,000.

The hospital continued to be concerned about providing the community with excellent medical care at a reasonable cost. The hospital now had 215 beds and the school of nursing had already graduated 172 nurses in its 17 years of existence.

*Pictures and
Personalities
from
"The Birth of
a Hospital"*

An early classroom and chapel at Baptist Sanitarium

The first graduating class of Baptist Sanitarium Training School in 1909.

A Business Section of Houston as seen from the Roof Garden of the Baptist Sanitarium

The Original Building after the Second Enlargement in 1914, which increased the 1911 addition to 8 stories.

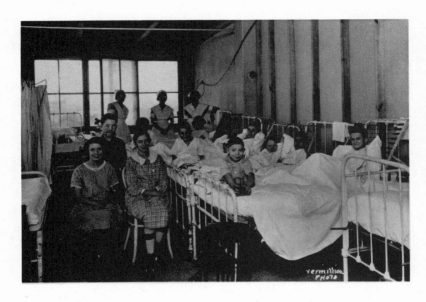

The Baby Camp, at the Top of the Sixth Floor
Wing of the Hospital

BAPTIST SANITARIUM OPERATING ROOM

The Laboratory Department in the early 1900's

DIET KITCHEN, FOURTH FLOOR; 1918

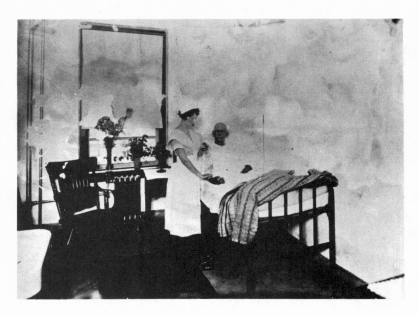

A PRIVATE ROOM IN 1918

View of the Baptist Sanitarium addition, as
seen from the corner of Smith and Dallas
Streets. The white cottage in front later
became the Children's Hospital.

PERSONALITY PROFILE:
JUDGE T. M. KENNERLY

Judge T. M. Kennerly was born in 1874, admitted to the Bar when he was 19 (because he was so young, special provisions were necessary); and appointed U. S. District Judge by President Hoover in 1931. He was a member of Second Baptist Church where he served as Chairman of the Board of Deacons. He was also a very well-known Christian educator; he taught a Bible class where the membership grew to 400 and his Sunday morning religious Broadcast was aired over two radio stations. He also wrote a Bible lesson for the *Houston Post*.

He was one of the founders of Memorial Hospital, and served on its Board of Trustees for over 50 years. For 20 of those years, he served as Chairman of the Board. During his years as a leader at Memorial, he helped develop the hospital from the original frame building to the Central complex of the 440-bed main building.

In March of 1961, the Board presented him with a plaque which honored his long service to the hospital. It read:

> *The Trustees of Memorial Baptist Hospital, in grateful appreciation of Thomas Martin Kennerly, member of the Board of Trustees since 1907, President of the Board for many years, for his Christian influence, wise leadership, faithful service, wise counseling, great vision, serving God and man.*

PERSONALITY PROFILE:
MRS. IDA J. RUDISILL

Mrs. Ida J. Rudisill saw the need for a hospital in Houston during the early part of this century and built the Rudisill Sanitarium which was sold in 1907 and became the Baptist Sanitarium. She stayed on to help with the management of the institution and to become the hospital's first Superintendent of Nursing. Miss Laura Irena Evans, the valedictorian of the first class of nurses, said this about Mrs. Rudisill in her address:

Our kind Superintendent, Mrs. Rudisill, by her precepts and example, has taught the lesson of a life devoted to a noble purpose, with the exclusion of anything that would prevent its fulfillment. We esteem it among the rarest of our present privileges that we are permitted to address a few words to one so noble and true. In no mere compliance with formal custom in behalf of our class do we tender to you our sincere gratitude for the helpful and sympathetic relations to us in the class in the year now closing.

During the groundbreaking ceremonies later that afternoon, Mrs. Rudisill and Mrs. Charles Stewart, aided by the architect, Mr. R. D. Steele, formally broke the soil for the first new wing of the hospital. Mrs. Rudisill resigned as Superintendent of Nursing late in 1911 or early in 1912.

PERSONALITY PROFILE:
REVEREND DENNIS ROBERT PEVOTO

The Reverend Dennis Robert Pevoto was born in 1873 near Johnson Bayou, Louisiana. At age 19, he became a schoolteacher; he saved his earnings from that position and went on to study at Liberty Normal Business College in Liberty Hill, Texas. He received his diploma from there one day in 1898, married on the next day, and then a series of events took him to Houston where, in 1900, he became Minister of the Clark Street Baptist Church.

In 1904 the Reverend Pevoto and the Reverend Mays began discussing the need for a church-related hospital in Houston. Then Reverend Pevoto, with the assistance of Dr. D. L. Gross, founded the hospital in 1907 and subsequently became the first Superintendent. He remained in that post until he left to work for the Baptist General Convention of Texas ten years later. During this period of his life he also founded, with the support of Mrs. Charles Stewart, and with financial help from Judge T. M. Kennerly and J. E. Burkhardt, the Star of Hope Mission at 714 Franklin Street. After working for the Convention, he became pastor of Baptist churches in Opelousas, Louisiana, and Brenham, Texas. He then went to San Angelo, Texas, as a hospital superintendent and from there to Beaumont, Texas, as a pastor. In his later years, he returned to Houston.

The force and humor of his personality perhaps come across best in the section of his autobiography which describes a severe case of pneumonia which befell him when

Continued on Page 42

PERSONALITY PROFILE
REV. PEVOTO
(Cont'd)

he returned to Houston for a visit in 1918. He was so sick that his physician, Dr. D. M. Lister, called Mrs. Lee, the hospital missionary, and told her that "Pevoto would have to have help that the world could not give." He did recover, however, and he described his departure from the hospital in this way:

> *On account of the fact that I founded the institution, shaped its policies, nursed it through its infancy and stayed with it for 10 years and 4 months, beginning on the magnificent salary of $75.00 per month, the new President and the new management agreed to deduct one-half my bill. I was so grateful for this magnificent favor that I proceeded to deduct the other half—acting upon the advice of several members of the Board of Directors who learned that a charge had been made.*

CHAPTER TWO

"The credit belongs to the man who is actually in the arena. . ."

—*THEODORE ROOSEVELT*

2

INNOVATION AND EXCELLENCE
1925 - 1948

Houston in the late 1920's and early 1930's began to take on some of the features which now characterize it as a city. In the year 1927, for example, the junior college which would grow into the multi-campus University of Houston was opened. And in 1930, that uniquely Houston institution—the Houston Rodeo—began. The institution that would become the Memorial Hospital System also began to take on a more definite shape during these years. The early years of fighting to survive were over; the hospital had established itself as an important part of the city. The rapid expansion of those early years was also over for a while.

Growth was still a very necessary goal, but the years following the Great Depression made capital fund-raising even more difficult. The hospital had excellent leadership during this period of hard times; people like Judge Kennerly and the Jollys worked hard and successfully not only to keep the hospital abreast of all the changes in medical technology and techniques, but also to keep its general funding high enough to provide excellent health care.

An editorial in *The Houston Press* on May 5, 1935, described the plight of Houston hospitals during these years.

Sunday, besides being Mother's Day, is National Hospital Day, which is celebrated each May 12 because that is the birthday of Florence Nightingale, the angel of the modern hospital.

Houston has a particular interest in the celebration of the day this year because Robert Jolly of our own Memorial Hospital is President of the American Hospital Association. He has gone to New York, where he will speak Sunday on the day and its significance over a nationwide radio chain.

Houstonians would do well to listen to Mr. Jolly. The plight of the private hospital— such as Memorial, St. Joseph's and Methodist—is acute. Perhaps no other American institution has been hit so hard by the depression.

The number of paying patients they have served has decreased while the charity patients have increased, thus lessening the income and increasing the expenses. In addition, the donations of the public and the income from endowments have fallen sharply.

. . . . . . We must have hospitals, but they cannot exist unless they earn their way or have large endowments to take care of their deficits. Let Houstonians study the problem. Perhaps there are some among us who can help.

Another editorial of the period, this one in *The Houston Post* in August of 1933, addressed the same nationwide problem and how it affected Texas.

Some of the private hospitals in New York are reporting mounting deficits. One is running in the red $80,000 per year, another $150,000 and another $200,000 per year. The situation is serious. These institutions must be *kept in operation. They render an indispensable service, but where to get the money to keep them going—that's the rub.*

New York hospitals have no monopoly on financial troubles. Some of the institutions in Texas have similar difficulties. Hard times have reduced patronage by paying patients, increased the number of patients unable to pay for service, and decreased gifts from people interested in the cause the hospitals serve.

The Baptist Sanitarium and Hospital attempted to meet this problem by changing its name. On January 1, 1932, after 25 years of service to the community, it became Memorial Hospital.

This change, which had been discussed even earlier in the hospital's history, and which was the forerunner of later efforts to make the hospital support base as broad as its service base, was announced by the Chairman of the Board of Directors, Judge T. M. Kennerly. He reported that the "new name was adopted in recognition of the many gifts of equipment and funds made in memory of relatives of Houston people." He also emphasized a point made by the newspaper editorials: the charity case load at the hospital was heavy, and it was given regardless of creed. He said that "only about 30 percent of the free service has been given to Baptists, while 20 percent has been given to members of other denominations and 50 percent to non-church members." Over its first 25 years of existence, the hospital had provided $500,000 in free service to the residents of Houston and South Texas. His concluding remarks urged the community to repay some of that support. Donations were necessary to the work of the hospital and "those interested in establishing memorials" could do so ". . . in connection with the hospital, where such memorials will benefit suffering humanity 24 hours a day for every day in the year."

This name change was like the separation from the Baptist Convention and the enlargement of the Board of Trustees which would become necessary some 30 years later. It reflected both the breadth of the hospital's service to the community, and the need for increased support from the broad population that it served.

This appeal for increased support did not mean, however, that there had been no support from the community. In fact, in August of 1928, Mr. and Mrs. J. W. Neal and their son, Robert J. Neal, Vice President of the Second National Bank, had established an important memorial fund. The trust, called the Margaret Ophelia Neal Trust Fund, was in memory of the Neals' daughter who died of meningitis at the age of two. This fund of $100,000 was used for the treatment of ill and disabled children. By 1937, some 614 children had been treated with the interest money from the fund. Mr. Neal, who was a longtime member and officer of the Board of Trustees, and Mrs. Neal, who was active in the Auxiliary, asked that careful records of each child helped by the trust be kept. The records of the children treated were kept on loose leaves and then bound into a book which recorded the beneficiaries of the trust. Mr. Neal called the book "our treasure book," and he kept it on a desk in his office.

Later in this period, the Neals established another memorial fund for the son, Robert, who died of cancer. This 1940 gift provided for the X-ray treatment of cancer victims.

"BABY-BREATHER" MACHINE

The Neals were not the only contributors to the hospital during this period. In 1931, Mr. Jolly announced that a donor, who chose to remain anonymous, had helped the hospital by purchasing for it a Drinker Respirator for children. This machine, developed by the famous Dr. Drinker of Harvard, was called a "baby breather," because it was used to resuscitate babies smothered at the time of birth and other babies too weak to breathe on their own. When this machine came to the hospital, the nearest one like it was in St. Louis, and there were only 36 machines like it in the entire United States and Canada. Mr. Jolly estimated that it could save as many as 50 lives a year in the Houston area.

Mr. Jolly also made use of this gift in another way, a way which helps characterize the style of the hospital administration during his years. When he announced the gift and its importance to the public, he concluded *The Houston Press* story with a reminder that the Houston area was still without a Drinker Respirator, or "iron lung," for adults. As he thanked the donor of the "baby breather," he expressed the hope that some other philanthropic citizen would present the hospital with an adult machine. Note that the inscription on the side of the machine (Page 54) states "Presented by a friend," with the donation date August 31, 1931. Mr. Jolly's public hint had worked; although times were hard, the hospital had its second machine just a scant six weeks after the first one.

In fact, Mr. Jolly's success in soliciting such funds shows that one of the hospital's chief assets during this period was his energetic salesmanship. The Houston newspapers for this period show Mr. Jolly as a civic leader who constantly spoke for the hospital before such groups as Rotary, the Optimists, and the Elks. He was, in quite a literal sense, a fast talker (one article clocked his speech at a number of words per minute which was equal to the fastest in the country), and he never stopped using his energy to represent the institution.

Mr. Jolly was also very adept at using the newspaper media to keep the community aware of the hospital's service to the community and its need for money. Newspaper articles, advertisements, and newsletter features of the time show him using his skills as an evangelistic storyteller to get the public's attention and to arouse public sympathy for Memorial's patients and its work. The reproduction (Pages 50 and 51) of the tale, "Eggs in a Flour Sack," with its tone of an evangelistic preacher's sermon and its documentary notation "(This child is now in the Memorial Hospital — Robert Jolly, Superintendent)" shows the way he worked.

Memorial had always worked hard to improve efficiency and cut costs, but the hospital made a special effort during these hard times to lower maternity care costs. The reduced rate in 1937 was $21.00 for a three-day stay in the ward and $27.00 for a private room. These charges, which were about 30 percent under the regular rates, included use of the birth room, care of the baby and use of the respirator. Mr. Jolly announced the reduced rates by commenting on the horrible

"EGGS IN A

About three months ago a man in overalls, evidently from the country, came to my office with a little 9-months-old boy in his arms and with his wife timidly following. It was so apparent they were frightened and ill at ease that I doubled my efforts to make them feel they were in the house of friendship.

Said he: "I live at Willow Springs and I work 37 acres of land which I have been trying to buy with my share of the crop. But I am behind on payments and have been on relief and only made 300 pounds of cotton last year. I owe one man $44 for money advanced me for living expenses. We have another child at home and we four are doing the best we can. A neighbor brought us down here in his car."

I looked out the window at the car and wondered how they ever got it over the road to Houston.

He showed me a cancer on the little child's hand about the size of a marble and said that the country doctor had told him he could do nothing for it, but to bring the child to Memorial Hospital and he was sure we would do whatever was needed for its removal.

I placed them in charge of a staff doctor who treated the cancer and told them to return in 30 days for another treatment. They went back into the piney woods country and at the appointed time returned with the child. The parents could hardly wait to get into my office to show me how greatly the cancer was reduced, and their joy and gratitude was touching. The doctor gave the child the second treatment and told them the cancer would shortly disappear but to come back in three months for observation.

When the child was dismissed the man came back to my office to tell me goodbye. He seemed to want to linger for something, but finally went out. In a few moments he was back with the child on one arm and in the other hand was clutched an old dirty flour sack about one-half full of something. The man seemed not to know just how to begin, but finally he managed to say: "There are three dozen eggs in this sack, each one wrapped in newspaper."

Before he could proceed, thinking he was about to offer the eggs for sale, and trying to make it easy for him, I blurted out, "Well, that's fine. How much do you want for them? We will be glad to buy them from you."

"No," he said. "I don't want to sell them. I want to give them to Memorial Hospital."

"But," I said, "you can't afford to give them to us. We can better afford to buy them from you than you can to give them to us and I would like to help you by purchasing them."

And then by the expression of his face and the tears in his eyes I knew I had said the wrong thing and had offended him.

In a trembling voice he replied, "No, sir, you would rob us of all the joy. We have 19 chickens which we really own and they laid these eggs. We have no other way to show Memorial Hospital how much we appreciate what

FLOUR SACK"

has been done for our little boy. Please let us give them to you as our only way of paying and thanking the hospital."

I then told him that a West Texas friend, who would not want his name used, had sent us some money to help just such cases and that it was a joy to the hospital to be of service in helping the child to get well, and in helping the friend to spend some money in such worth-while manner.

I accepted the eggs and his tears turned to smiles as he and his wife and baby started back to their piney woods home.

BUT—

A few days ago they brought the baby back. This time he is desperately ill with typhus fever and our doctors and nurses are pitting their skill against this disease that has fastened itself upon this little fellow.

The mother tells me today that they are having to give up their little farm home because of non-payment. They did not make enough cotton to offer for sale. She and the father came in my office to tell me they have to go back today to get their few possessions out of the house and into some other place.

Said she: "We just could not leave the little fellow if we did not believe you folks would do your best for him."

(This child is now in Memorial Hospital—Robert Jolly, Superintendent)

(We will do our best for this unfortunate child, and we could take care of hundreds of such children and make other hearts happy if we had the money and facilities)

WOULD YOU LIKE A PART IN THIS GREAT WORK?

─────────── YOU ───────────

With others could give as a memorial, a BABIES' AND CHILDREN'S BUILDING in which to care for new born babies, and sick and disabled children.

DO YOU KNOW OF ANY GREATER MONUMENT
YOU COULD LEAVE TO YOUR MEMORY?

• *GIVING IS LIVING* •

MEMORIAL HOSPITAL

"It Is More Blessed to Give Than to Receive"

infant mortality record held by the United States. "It is a startling fact that in this enlightened age and in our prosperous country more women between the ages of 15 and 45 lose their lives from conditions connected with childbirth than from any other cause except tuberculosis. In Houston last year, 109 babies died before they were one month old, and only last month 18 died before they reached the age of a month."

Mr. Jolly went on to say that "One-half of the babies who die, die before they are six weeks old, and these deaths are due largely to the condition of the mothers and the lack of proper care and attention during and following confinement." He was optimistic, however, that "prospective parents are more and more turning to the hospital as the place for their children to be born." He said that in 1920, when he became superintendent at Memorial, only 20 percent of the babies born in Houston were born in hospitals. In 1931 the figure was 64 percent, and recently it had gone up to 71 percent. Mr. Jolly concluded this educational presentation with the belief "that when the depression is over we shall see a still further increase in the percentage of babies born in the hospital."

Memorial, in the meantime, was doing its best to educate the public about the values of hospital maternity care and to make that care available even during the depression years.

Mr. Jolly's energetic advancement of health care education and of the hospital took other forms as well. Early in the hospital's history, the Reverend Pevoto had traveled throughout the country to learn more about health care practices and hospital management. Mr. Jolly continued and expanded this tradition of national interest and involvement. At this time, many national health care organizations were just being founded or were just beginning to grow into significant membership and influence. Mr. Jolly was a national leader in such health management organizations. *The Houston Press* article quoted earlier mentions his presidency in 1935 of the American Hospital Association, but it should be added that Mr. Jolly was the first man from the South to hold that office. He was also made a charter fellow of the prestigious American College of Hospital Administrators.

During the same years that he spoke so often before churches and clubs here, Mr. Jolly also spoke around the country. Newspapers of the time record his appearances before lay and professional groups in Cleveland, Minneapolis, Philadelphia, Louisville and other cities. This national recognition helped Memorial become known as an important and progressive hospital, and it also made sure that Mr. Jolly and others at the hospital were aware of all the latest developments in medicine.

There were many such changes during the Jolly years at Memorial. During the 1920's the electrocardiograph and the electroencephalogram were introduced as diagnostic procedures, and there was a lab procedure established for determining the Basal Metabolism Rate. Insulin eliminated diabetes as a hospital disease, liver extract controlled pernicious anemia, and an immunization for diphtheria was developed.

Memorial incorporated all of these developments and made other changes as well. The school of nursing, for example, began teaching psychology. Dieticians and pharmacists were added to the employee roster. There was also an increase in the amount of surgery performed, much of it being done to correct nutritional deficiencies in children. Mr. Jolly worked very hard to make sure that Memorial had the latest medical knowledge and technology, and to make sure that all such advances were, like Memorial's maternity services, made known to the Houston public. An article in *The Houston Chronicle*, for example, featured the Memorial Hospital slogan of the period, "Always Ready," and spotlighted a collection of the newer medical devices at the hospital.

The group of devices included the first item pictured on Page 54. Although the photograph makes it look foreboding, the device is only a bronchoscope used to remove foreign objects from the throat. Other machines were Memorial's new electrocardiograph, and an electro-magnet, used to remove steel particles from the eye and thus to cut down on the need for surgery. Also pictured in this 1932 newspaper article was a second "baby breather." This machine was still another donation to the hospital, given

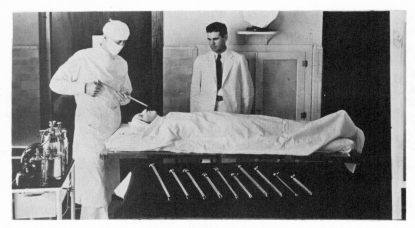

THE NEW BRONCHOSCOPE

THE IRON LUNG DONATED IN 1931

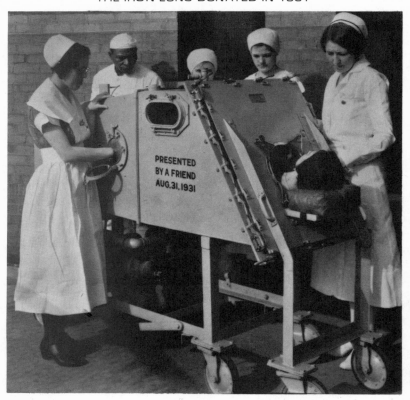

PRESENTED
BY A FRIEND
AUG. 31, 1931

because there were periods when two babies needed a machine at the same time.

Medical equipment was one important feature which Memorial offered the Houston community, but there were others too, and one of the most important of these was its tradition of personal care. This can be seen in an interview with Mrs. Lillie Wilson Burnett Jolly in 1938, her 30th year at the hospital and school. She looked back on important events during her years at the hospital and recalled the trauma of the race riot during World War I, the great hurricane of 1915, and the big thrill of seeing the first four floors of the new addition go up in 1924.

She recalled especially how they "had worked so long in the little building, crowded and handicapped." During that time "we worked all day and had our school at night," and since there was no house doctor, school often had to be interrupted while "a baby was brought safely into the world."

For Mrs. Jolly, however, these moments of high drama and triumph were not the most important parts of her job. She speaks for many Memorial employees over the years when she said that what made hospital life "fascinating" was "the fact that every day we can help somebody in some way.... I like to work with the girls in the school of nursing and help the girl who has not had opportunities to find herself get started on the right track. I like the contacts with the patients —the little human things that inevitably result from these contacts."

The last part of the 1930's brought the beginning of substantial changes in how an individual could pay for health care. Baylor Hospital of Dallas had put in place a health insurance plan (now known as Blue Cross) in 1927; by 1939, it had some 28,000 members, all of whom paid a monthly fee for insurance to cover major medical costs. In 1939, a bill in the Texas State Legislature in Austin proposed to extend this plan so that laborers and middle-class people could receive hospitalization coverage. Although hospital leaders encouraged "heads of households to take sickness into account in making up their family's annual budget," insurance did not really become common until group coverage became popular almost 20 years later.

The 1940's brought another period of rapid development in medical skills and in the need both for new kinds of patient care and new kinds of medical education. In the early 1940's, for example, student nurses needed to know the names of about 25 common drugs. By the 1970's, the number increased to over 300. Nurse education was also expanding to include more subjects outside the basic nursing. To make sure that their nurses got a good broad general education, the Memorial school entered into an affiliation with the University of Houston in 1940. Memorial received the first shipment of the new "wonder" drug penicillin in 1943, and it was also the first general hospital in Houston to provide psychiatric care.

As the country moved away from the depression era, Houston was still growing and Memorial needed to keep pace. In early 1941, the Board of Trustees had to decide whether to enlarge the hospital or to build a building for the nursing school. Both needs were pressing. But financing both would have to be done by going into debt, and this meant that only one could be built. The Board chose the building which would enlarge the bed capacity, secured financing from the Massachusetts Mutual Life Insurance Company, and began the eight-story addition on Smith and Dallas in 1941. When it was completed in 1942, this new addition brought the bed capacity of Memorial up to 284. It also provided new quarters for the X-ray department and the Pathology laboratory, and it enlarged the areas available for the dietary department and for nursing education.

A NEW BUILDING; A NEW SCHOOL OF NURSING

Subsequent events, however, made it possible for Memorial to have its nurses' building too. In the 1940's, the war greatly increased the country's demand for medical personnel. And after the war, the need—especially the need for nurses— continued. To help Memorial educate more nurses, three benefactors donated what became the Lillie Jolly School of Nursing. In 1944, Mrs. Neal gave the hospital $175,000 for the

56

purchase of the entire city block across Lamar from the hospital, and specified that her gift be used for a school of nursing and dormitory. Then, one year later, Mr. and Mrs. Hugh Roy Cullen gave the hospital $1 million to construct the building. They followed that initial gift with a second $1 million to complete the building, plus additional money to cover the original land cost. That same year, 1945, the name of the school was changed to the Lillie Jolly School of Nursing, in honor of its longtime Superintendent, Mrs. Jolly. When the new building was completed in 1948, it was named the Cullen Nurses Building. The new building fulfilled a dream held by Mrs. Jolly since the 1920's. Its new facilities and accommodations finally gave the school that she had built accommodations which were equal to the quality of its education.

The completion of the new building in 1948 also served to mark the end of an era in the history of Memorial Hospital. Mr. Jolly retired in 1946, and Mrs. Jolly retired soon after in 1947. After more than 68 combined years of leadership for the institution, they left behind a vastly changed Memorial Hospital. It had a fine hospital building which could accommodate the recent advances in medical technology, and it had a new nurses' building with up-to-date facilities. It also had a 40-year tradition of medical service to a still growing Houston community.

When new leaders came in at the end of the Jolly era, they came to a healthy institution. Mr. John G. Dudley assumed the leadership of the hospital in 1946 as Hospital Administrator, and two years later Miss Daisy Moore became Nursing Administrator.

25,000
Babies Can't Be Wrong

There are a few shining hours in life.
A few hours when worldly wisdom falls
away, like so much veneer, and funda-
mentals are clear and bright. During
these hours you and your baby are the
center of a small, protected universe.
Only the things that concern YOU are
really important.

MEMORIAL HOSPITAL and the entire
personnel of our Maternity Department
stand ready to focus their attention and
efforts upon you and your needs in
those shining hours

More than 25,000 babies have been
born in Memorial Hospital.

"Always Ready"

Maternity
Department

MEMORIAL HOSPITAL
602 LAMAR AVENUE ✦ HOUSTON

Above: Christmas Eve 1937 in Front of "The
Little White Cottage." Below: Maternity
Care ad.

Memorial Hospital as it looked in the 1930's (above) and as it looked in the early 1940's (below), after still another enlargement.

Above: 1942 newspaper photo of two visiting hospital administrators with Mr. Walter Walne, Chairman of the Building Committee (2nd from left) and Mr. Robert Jolly (2nd from right). Below: Mr. Hugh Roy Cullen signing $1 million check which he gave for Cullen Nurses' Building in 1945. Left to right, Mr. F. M. Law, Mrs. Cullen and Mr. Robert Jolly.

PERSONALITY PROFILE:
MR. AND MRS. J. W. NEAL

Colonel J. W. Neal and his wife, Elizabeth Mitchell Neal, were outstanding Houston citizens, church members, and philanthropists. Colonel Neal, born in Fountain Run, Kentucky, became interested in the coffee business while working with a wholesale grocery in Nashville, Tennessee. In 1896, he organized (with Joel Cheek) the Cheek-Neal Coffee Company, which made Maxwell House Coffee famous. In 1903 Col. Neal visited Texas looking for possible places to expand his company. He prophesied that Houston was destined to be the largest city in the Southwest and opened a branch of the company here. He moved his family to Houston and began to take a prominent part in civic and church affairs. In 1928 he sold the company to General Foods. Soon after, he bought a controlling interest in the Second National Bank and became Chairman of its Board.

He was a Deacon in the First Baptist Church and, with his wife, helped organize the Second Baptist Church. He served on a vast number of civic and philanthropic organizations including the Y.M.C.A., the Community Chest, the Chamber of Commerce, and the Rotary Club. In 1928 he was presented with the Rotary medal given annually to a Houstonian for the most unselfish service rendered that year.

Shortly after coming to Houston he was made a Trustee of Memorial Hospital; he was Executive Vice-President of the Board for five years, and President of the Board from 1938 until his death in 1940. Outstanding among the philanthropies of Colonel and Mrs. Neal were the gifts to Memorial Hospital. They created two trust funds in memory of their children: the Margaret Ophelia Neal Fund for sick and disabled children was created in memory of their daughter; and the James Robert Neal Fund for the X-ray treatment of cancer was created in memory of their son.

PERSONALITY PROFILE:
MR. ROBERT JOLLY

Mr. Robert Jolly was born in Cave City, Kentucky. He was interested in church work, especially in evangelistic singing, even as a young man; but his first job was that of an Auditor of the L. & N. Railroad. He began work as an evangelist in 1906, and was in evangelistic work for seven years before he became assistant to the pastor of Gaston Avenue Church in Dallas. He stayed there for four years before taking a similar position with Dr. J. B. Leavell of the First Baptist Church in Houston. Shortly thereafter, he became Business Manager, and then Superintendent, of the hospital.

As Superintendent, he saw that the Houston hospital could develop because of contacts with others and he began to take an interest in national hospital organizations. In 1920 he was elected President of the American Protestant Hospital Association. In 1925 he was First Vice President of the American Hospital Association, and in 1933, President of the Texas Hospital Association. When the American College of Hospital Administrators was organized in 1933, he was made a charter member and a member of its Board of Governors. That same year, he achieved what might have been his most significant national post. He was made President-elect (to serve as President from 1934 to 1935) of the American Hospital Association. He was the fourth layman ever to be elected to this position (all others had been physicians), and was the first man from the South to hold the title of President in the 36-year history of the organization.

Continued on Page 64

PERSONALITY PROFILE:
MRS. LILLIE JOLLY

Mrs. Lillie Jolly came to work at the Baptist Sanitarium and Nursing School soon after her graduation from the School of Nursing at the Kentucky School of Medicine. Miss Lillian Wilson, as she was known then, was somewhat surprised by the cramped quarters, and she recalls that "I felt like shouting to the hack driver to take me back to the depot." She stayed, however, and during her 40-year career at the hospital, helped to build the nursing school into a major institution.

She became Superintendent of Nurses in 1911 or 1912 and held that position for the rest of her career. Although she was active in nursing affairs, serving as President of the Texas League of Nursing Educators, and on the Nursing Committee of the American Hospital Association, her main contribution was the development of the nursing school.

On January 1, 1924, she married Mr. Robert Jolly, Hospital Superintendent, and they presided over the growth and development of the school and hospital for the next 20 years. In 1942 Mr. F. M. Law, Treasurer of the Board, said to her: "I wish to congratulate not so much you, but the hospital, on being able to have you during these 35 years." Mr. A. D. Foreman, Board Chairman, elaborated some on this when acknowledging her 38th anniversary of work there. "Mrs. Jolly occupies a most enviable position in the profession of nursing, not only because she has a thorough mastery of the intricate scientific features of the profession, but also because she has the wonderful faculty of inspiring." From the first

Continued on Page 64

PERSONALITY PROFILE
ROBERT JOLLY
(Cont'd)

Mr. Jolly was a member of the South Main Baptist Church. He was a Deacon, a member of the finance committee, and a frequent leader of evangelistic meetings there and elsewhere.

On January 1, 1924, Mr. Jolly and Mrs. Lillie Burnett were married, and together they managed the hospital and the nursing school for the next 20 years. During the Jollys' leadership, the hospital added much-needed new equipment, became certified by the American College of Surgeons, and expanded its facilities greatly.

PERSONALITY PROFILE
LILLIE JOLLY
(Cont'd)

class of nine graduates in 1909 until her retirement in 1947, more than 900 nurses graduated under her supervision. In 1945, the nursing school was renamed The Lillie Jolly School of Nursing, in honor of her years of work and accomplishments.

CHAPTER THREE

Cultivate a pleasing personality, give the best there is in you, and never overlook an opportunity to improve, or learn something new.

THE SCHOOL OF NURSING

Would you rather be a so-called flapper nurse (short hair, short skirt, pink hose and gray shoes, beads, rings and rouge) or the dignified, professional nurse in the proper uniform? Which of these would you choose to nurse your mother?

This quote, taken from *RULES AND STANDARDS FOR STUDENT NURSES*, printed in 1926 and written by the Superintendent of Nurses, Mrs. Robert Jolly, exemplifies the high standards and professionalism demanded of the students at the Baptist Hospital School of Nursing. These standards of excellence have been a cornerstone of this school, from its founding until its incorporation with Houston Baptist University.

The year 1907 was a significant one in the Houston medical field, for not only was it the year the Baptist Hospital was founded, but also the year the first chartered school of nursing in Houston was established—the Baptist Sanitarium Training School.

The school was chartered and established by hospital founder Rev. D. R. Pevoto, and Mrs. Ida J. Rudisill, who had been the original owner of the hospital. Ten students entered the training program at that time, and two years later, seven graduated. The training program, though only two years long, was a very arduous one. A second-year student nurse worked a six-and-a-half-day week, from 7:00 a.m. to 7:00 p.m. (or 7:00 p.m. to 7:00 a.m. if she were on night duty), and was also required to attend chapel at 6:45 every morning. Qualifications for admission obviously included stamina, as well as a sixth-grade education and the ability to pass exams in reading, writing, spelling and arithmetic. A student applicant was also required to present a certificate of health from a physician and a certificate of character from a pastor.

In these early days, the teachers in the nursing school were actually the hospital doctors, who delivered lectures between rounds and emergencies. If there was no one available to instruct the students on health care, they were given Bible study courses. This was not merely a means of passing time, for each girl in this program was required to obtain a Sunday School Teachers' Certificate along with her diploma in nursing. This prerequisite was, as Rev. Pevoto noted, unique with the nursing school, and further illustrates the high standards that were always a part of the school.

The first students did not live at home, but next door to the hospital with the Pevoto family. They attended chapel services daily, and church on Sundays, and even made their own uniforms. Certainly no dating was allowed, so that these two years of a student nurse's life were almost a complete immersion in preparing her for her place in life. A girl with the strength of character and perseverance to complete her training would surely become a dedicated professional, one for whom "the patient always comes first."

The concept of nursing during those early days of this century was entirely different than it is now. The nurses of the early 1900's understood that they were simply to follow orders, and that the doctor's word was to be unquestioned. It was similar to the military in many respects, probably due to the fact that nursing schools of the day were patterned after the Florence Nightingale schools in Europe, which were founded on Miss Nightingale's experience as an Army nurse. A "concept of medicine" was not taught, other than that of the patient's comfort. Indeed, at that time, making the patient comfortable in a clean and efficient environment was often the best that could be done. The primary function of nurses was the performance of rather menial tasks, such as washing bedpans, changing beds, rolling bandages, cleaning patients' rooms; boiling syringes, surgical instruments and gloves, and keeping records and charts. These duties are now handled by LVNs, orderlies, nurses' aides and others trained specifically for these tasks.

At the Baptist Sanitarium, each nurse had under her care eight to ten patients. During the course of her 12-hour day, she carried out all the duties listed previously, as well as fixing meal trays for them from the kitchen located on each floor. Because patients stayed in the hospital three to four weeks in those days (even for minor ailments), a nightly rub was a prerequisite in the constant battle against bedsores. The nurse was allowed to mix and measure the medications prescribed by the doctors, although not permitted to give injections, and before she could call her day complete, it was imperative that she fill out a report of all functions performed for each patient under her care.

The ensuing years saw a small, though steady, increase in enrollment in the school of nursing. Students lived in whatever accommodations could be found near the hospital. As the school and the hospital grew, students lived in various houses in the vicinity. One of these, pictured on Page 72 , was purchased from the King family and so became called "King House." Naturally, the second house purchased had to be called "Queen House." This arrangement continued for 40 years, until the Cullen Nurses Building was completed in 1947. By that time, the school of nursing had been long established as one of the leading nursing schools in the United States.

LILLIAN WILSON JOLLY

In the same year that the Baptist Sanitarium and Training School were founded, a young woman graduated from the School of Nursing at the Kentucky School of Medicine. In 1908, at the urging of a friend, she applied for a position with the Baptist Sanitarium, and was accepted. She arrived in Houston that year to begin work as a surgeon's assistant and then, three years later, as Director of Nurses. Her name was Miss Lillian Wilson, and later, as Mrs. Robert Jolly, she was to shape the character of the school.

During her first three years of employment at the Baptist Sanitarium, Miss Wilson proved herself to be extremely capable and versatile. She adroitly performed every function and duty necessary. In addition to her job as surgical nurse, she was also, at times, day superintendent, night superintendent, supervisor of obstetrics and surgery, housekeeper and dietician, and often carried out many of these duties simultaneously. The experience she acquired during this nascent period in the hospital's history proved invaluable over the next three decades. Somewhere around the end of 1911 or early 1912, Mrs. Rudisill, the founder of the original sanitarium, resigned her position as Superintendent of Nurses, justifiably proud of the 16 fine young nurses the school had graduated up to that time. Miss Wilson was named as her replacement, and thus began this remarkable woman's influence on the school.

As the school expanded, the need for a more extensive curriculum in the nursing school became apparent.

In 1914, the program was increased from two years to three. Students were drawn to the school from all over the state, as well as from Louisiana and Arkansas, and although there was only one graduate in 1915, the overall enrollment remained steady. In 1916, the first full-time instructor was added: Miss Retta Johnson, R.N. She was only one of ten full-time nursing instructors throughout the entire United States, as most courses were still being taught by physicians during their off-hours.

In this same year, on April 13, the Alumnae Association was formed, and is still active to this day. The objectives of the organization are to promote the professional activities of its members, to work for the interests of the school of nursing, and to function as a representative group of professional graduate nurses.

In 1917, Rev. Pevoto resigned as Superintendent of the hospital, and in January 1918, Miss Wilson, who was now Mrs. Lillian Wilson Burnett, was named to this positon. She served in this capacity until 1920, when Mr. Robert Jolly, then acting as Business Manager, became Superintendent. Mrs. Burnett, who "disliked the business end of the work," was able to return to her first love, nursing, and to the tiny school where she could once again be with "her girls."

No one could better have exemplified the highest ideals of

the nursing profession, than Mrs. Jolly. When she first entered the little two-story hospital with its 18 beds, she in her own words, "felt like catching the first train home. But, when I saw how desperate the situation was, I decided to remain here and do what I could to help." Mrs. Burnett seems to have understated her intentions, for as we know, she filled every office in the hospital and was on call 24 hours a day. She slept in the the hospital, getting up at any hour of the night to assist in maternity cases, or wherever else she may have been needed. In fact, her dedication appears to have set the tone for the next several decades of the hospital's history. The staff of what was later to be called Memorial Hospital, became known for its personal concern and its devotion and commitment to "getting the job done."

This tradition of dedication to the patients' welfare was the foundation for the training school's teaching curriculum. The graduate nurses carried these ideals with them, whether or not they remained at the hospital to begin their nursing careers. Many of them did stay. But during both World Wars, many of the girls entered the military and served their country. In the second war alone, 97 graduate nurses volunteered for duty overseas. This was always a source of pride for Mrs. Jolly, as were those students who became missionaries in foreign lands. For along with devotion to the patient, she also liked to instill in her girls pride in country and love of God.

POST-WAR CHANGES

After World War I, the field of medicine had begun to grow in complexity. This was reflected in changes taking place at the institution. For instance, psychology was introduced into the curriculum in 1920, and even though it was not a significant part of the school's courses of study, it did indicate a movement toward a broader concept of health care. In 1921, the name of the school was changed to the Baptist Hospital School of Nursing, and then in 1923, it was decided that a high school diploma would be a requirement for admission to the program.

71

One of the Early Homes used for Students of
the School of Nursing

PARLOR IN NURSES' QUARTERS

NURSES STUDYING IN LIBRARY

While all these changes were being made, some other changes were taking place with the two chief administrators of the hospital and the nursing school. At a New Year's Eve Watch Party held at South Main Baptist Church to bring in 1924, Mrs. Burnett and Mr. Jolly surprised their staff and friends by handing the pastor a marriage license. They were then married at the stroke of 12. To those in attendance, it probably seemed the next logical step, as the hospital and the school had always been so closely allied in bringing the best health care possible to the city of Houston. For the next 25 years, the Jollys worked tirelessly to achieve this goal.

In September of 1924, the new addition to the hospital was opened and the school was enlarged to an enrollment of 100 students. The old hospital building was then turned into the nurses' home, after being moved across the street, and a story and basement added on. With the increase in enrollment came a need for more faculty members, so in 1929 two more full-time instructors were hired by the school.

Now, in addition to the instructors, the school was able to boast 12 supervisors, a music teacher and a Bible teacher. The music teacher, Miss Ella Musgrove, who served in this capacity for 20 years, organized the Glee Club in 1927, one of the first nurses' glee clubs in the United States. Her sister, Miss Emma Musgrove, who had been the hospital missionary for 20 years, conducted the student chapel services each morning. By now, the school also had its own full-fledged yearbook, *The Nightingale,* which was begun in 1918 and published every year except 1922. The name of the yearbook changed over the years, but a glance at later issues reveals that the well-rounded education and rich experiences shared by the young women who went through the nursing program at the Baptist Hospital School of Nursing stayed the same.

The year 1929 was also the last one in which Mrs. Jolly wore her nursing uniform. The school had grown so much that a full-time administrator was required, and Mrs. Jolly had no choice but to give up her nursing career to oversee all the activities of the school. So thorough was she that she even designed the cap worn by the students and graduates, and also set down the rules and principles which guided the school through the remainder of its existence. Here are the most characteristic of her guidelines, taken from the same *RULES AND STANDARDS FOR STUDENT NURSES* mentioned at the beginning of this chapter:

> *The patient must be considered first.*

> *It is the little things that count, and the thoughtful nurse will always know how to make a patient comfortable. . .*

> *Cultivate a pleasing personality, give the best there is in you, and never overlook an opportunity to improve, or learn something new.*

> *Your best is none too good, and no matter how much is required, always give a little more; every day do something that you do not want to do; make yourself do something difficult, something that is an effort.*

As medical technology expanded and the population of the United States became better educated, the nursing school realized the necessity to extend its curriculum. In 1940, it affiliated with the University of Houston, and courses in physical and biological sciences, nutrition and English were added. Classes in social sciences were also taught, reflecting both the growing complexity of American society and the need for nurses to know more about their patients.

In 1945, the school was renamed the Lillie Jolly School of Nursing, and in that same year, Mr. and Mrs. Hugh Roy Cullen quietly donated $1 million for the erection, equipment and furnishing of a new nurses' building. Mrs. Jolly's most fervent wish for "her girls" was to come true. The Cullens wanted to encourage young women to enter nursing, and by the time the new building was dedicated in July of 1948, they had donated another $1 million toward this facility. At last the student nurses had modern, spacious living quarters, and well-equipped classrooms in which to learn special skills.

Mrs. Jolly retired in June 1947, bringing to an end 40 truly remarkable years of service to the community and the nursing profession. Her place was taken by Miss Daisy Moore, who had worked closely with Mrs. Jolly since 1933. Miss Moore and her successors brought the Lillie Jolly School into the second half of the Twentieth Century, constantly updating the program, but always retaining the guiding principles set forth by Mrs. Jolly.

In 1966, the affiliation with the University of Houston was dissolved, and two years later, the school affiliated with Houston Baptist College. Two years of college work were now made a requirement for admission. When the new hospital building was opened in southwest Houston in 1972, the downtown hospital and the nurses building were closed. The Lillie Jolly School was incorporated into Houston Baptist University. This brought to an end the School of Nursing as a separate entity.

Even though student nurses of today graduate with an amount of knowledge equivalent to the doctors of 1907, and are far more advanced technologically, the basic requirements and standards of the nursing profession remain essentially unchanged. Mrs. Jolly's definition of the ideal nurse still holds:

I want to give you a picture of the nurse at her best. She is the woman physically strong and mentally alert, who thinks clearly and observes accurately; her sympathies are tender and at the same time, purposeful; her response to routine duties is competency, and to emergencies, initiative and resourcefulness. To all these qualities is added the lovely virtue, courage, through which not only her own life is made beautiful, but by means of which she inspires those to whom she administers.

Miss Daisy Moore stayed as Superintendent of the school from 1947 to 1955, and then Miss Barbara Odom was in charge from 1956 to 1957. Dr. Glendola Nash became Director in 1958 and kept that post until the nursing school moved to become part of Houston Baptist University. She became Dean of the College of Science and Health Professions at that University, and she still holds this position.

The Cullen Nurses' Building
Memorial Hospital

BAPTIST HOSPITAL
HOUSTON, TEXAS

Miss _Dorthy T Kleinhardt_

Your application for admission to the School of Nursing of the Baptist Hospital, Houston, Texas, has been received, considered and found satisfactory. You are therefore offered the position of Probationer.

The date of your coming will be _Sept 1st 1926_ If, however, other accepted candidates should fail to keep their appointments, the date of your coming may be hastened.

You are required to bring with you the following articlets: Four complete changes of underclothing, two pairs of comfortable shoes, biack, with rubber heels, and a watch with a second hand.

During entire time, including probation, you will wear the Training School uniform, as furnished.

You are required to deposit $10.00 with the cashier. This is to pay for uniform material, also the making of the probation uniform.

Your teeth must be in good conditon before coming to the Institution. Also, MUST BE SUCCESSFULLY VACCINATED.

If anything occurs to prevent you from keeping the above engagement, or there is a change in your address, you will kindly notify me at once.

Please answer immediately, stating whether you accept the vacancy occurring on the above date. If so, arrange to be here in the A. M. not later than 9.30 of the date you are to come, and come direct to the Hospital, sending your baggage also.

Mrs Robert Gilligan
SUPERINTENDENT OF NURSING

DATE _Aug 3rd 1926_

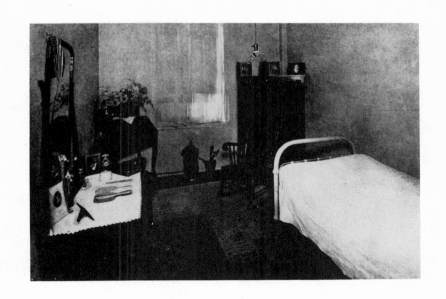

A NURSE'S ROOM IN THE 1920's

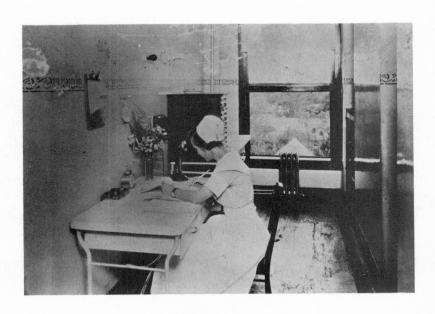

NURSING STATION IN THE 1920's

Mrs. Jolly in Conference with Nurses; Miss Daisy Moore is at right.

Early Morning Chapel for Student Nurses in the 1940's

UNCLE SAM NEEDS NURSES

NURSE RECEIVING HER CAP

The Army and Navy cannot secure enough nurses to supply the need for the National Defense Program. The need will increase each year.

Why not enroll in a Christian School of Nursing and be prepared for one of the 50 different classifications of nursing?

Nursing is a permanent career which will still be profitable when the war is over and the girl workers in War Industries will be hunting new jobs and perhaps even be having to learn new skills.

United States nurses go to every battlefront and will probably be called upon to handle vast problems in devastated areas after the war. "Be a nurse and see the world."

High School graduates between ages of 17 and 35 with required number of credits are eligible.

Write for Information to

MRS. ROBERT JOLLY, R.N., Director,

MEMORIAL HOSPITAL SCHOOL OF NURSING

Houston, Texas

NURSE CRISIS

81

Entrance and side view
of the new
Cullen Nurses' Building
taken in the 1950's.

CHAPTER FOUR

"When change is rapid and problems abundant, society must be creatively adaptive or fall further and further behind."

—*DAVID MOSS*

THE HOSPITAL AND THE CITY

The decade of the 1950's saw the maturing of the city and the hospital. As Houston expanded its port and road facilities to accommodate an expanding population, Memorial Hospital continued its record of rapid growth. In the 1950's, as in earlier years, Memorial grew in quality as well as numbers. For example, in this, its Golden Anniversary decade, Memorial Hospital added an outpatient clinic, a new technology school, a new professional building, and a program in psychiatry. The continuance of this tradition stemmed in large part from continued excellence in administration.

The history of any hospital will be, to a large extent, not only a history of the area it serves, but also a history of those who work for it. This is especially true of the Board of Trustees who help with planning and of the administrators who hire other employees and who set the public image, the tone, and the direction of the institution. Thus it was fortunate that when Mr. Jolly retired in 1946, Mr. John Gant Dudley soon became the hospital's administrator. After a brief period of six months, during which Mr. A. D. Foreman, Chairman of the Board of Trustees, occupied the position of administrator, Mr. Dudley moved to Houston.

As a hospital administrator in Arkansas, Mr. Dudley had toured hospitals in the Southwest to study the manner in which their emergency room facilities operated. Memorial was one place he visited, and he made a favorable impression on those who met him. He, however, had comfortably settled his wife and family into life in Arkansas, so that when Memorial first called him he did not want to move. He had liked the hospital on his visit here, though, so when they called again he listened. He did come to Memorial in 1946, and brought to the hospital later a very able associate and successor in Mr. W. Wilson Turner. Mr. Dudley's efficiency, his organizational abilities, and his genuine devotion to the hospital and its employees would add an important part to Memorial's history.

LAND OF OPPORTUNITY

Houston in the 1950's was a city preparing to take its place among other important cities in the country. The glories of older cities, such as New York and Chicago, were beginning to tarnish, as overcrowding and its inevitable consequences became more critical. People were just beginning to look toward the Southwest as the land of opportunity and promise. And as they turned their attention in this direction, they focused more and more on Houston.

Crucial to this burgeoning interest in Houston was the Ship Channel. By 1948, the Houston Ship Channel had moved from fourth place in the nation in tonnage handled, to second, ranking only behind New York. The port held this position until 1955, when it slipped to fourth place again, even though the facilities were being fully used. The need for expansion and improvement was apparent, so in 1957, bonds to allow for these needs were voted and passed. Shortly thereafter, the Port of Houston advanced to third position in the nation, where it remains. Although the major exports from the ship channel were, and still are grains, the most significant imports were crude oil and oil-related products. It was primarily this industry that set Houston on its course as one of the nation's leading cities.[1]

During the 1950's, railroad services declined in Houston and throughout the nation. Along with this came an emphasis on other means of shipping and transportation, primarily air travel and road travel. Thus, in 1954, Houston International Airport (later changed to Hobby Airport) opened on a site southeast of the city. It served six major

---

[1] This material on the city of Houston comes from David G. McComb's excellent urban history, *Houston: A History* (Austin, Texas). See especially Chapters 4, 5, and 6 which provided much of the information here.

airlines, two small companies, and one air freight line. At this time, although there were some international flights in and out of Houston, the city was restricted to north-south routes by the Civil Aeronautics Board. In 1956, however, the city was given its first eastern route. The following year, for the first time, a foreign carrier, KLM, began service between Houston and Europe, soon followed by a French carrier. Houston was becoming an international city.

In 1958 a delegation from Houston was able to wrest from the CAB air routes to California. This was significant because Houston now became a principal station between California and Florida, and an east-west flow of air traffic was now completed. Three years after the airport was opened, it was operating at peak capacity. Plans were being drawn up for the construction of a new facility northeast of the city. Houston was already having difficulties keeping up with its growth.

Major improvements in the roads and highways of Texas had been made during the 1930's, thanks to the Works Progress Administration. This allowed not only for greater ease in passenger travel, but also a growth in bus and truck lines, thereby contributing to the further decline of the railroads. By the beginning of the decade, there were nine bus lines coming into Houston, and trucking operations had increased as well.

THE GULF FREEWAY

The next step in Houston's growth was a major revamping and expanding of the highways, streets and roads in and around Houston. First to be completed was the Washburn Tunnel, linking Pasadena and the Ship Channel. Then the Gulf Freeway, between Houston and Galveston, was built in 1952, about the same time that a survey showed that all Houston highways should be four lanes wide. Plans were drawn up for the construction of a freeway system that would encircle the entire city, and work began on this enormous project in 1957. In the following decade, this massive freeway interchange would play a major role in Memorial Hospital's expansion.

Memorial Hospital had always been a vital part of the history of Houston, since its founding in 1907. It was inevitable, then, that the rapid growth and changes taking place in the city would be reflected in the hospital. In the early 1950's, Memorial had recognized the need for some kind of facility to accommodate the many people who needed treatment for minor illnesses, and the diagnosis of a particular problem, but who did not need extended hospitalization. Thus, in April of 1956, Memorial Hospital opened an Outpatient Department, containing both diagnostic and specialty clinics.

Under the supervision of a medical and hospital staff committee, the department conducted diagnostic clinics two mornings a week, for which patients made an appointment except in emergency cases. Members of the professional staff gave their time free of charge, and the patients paid according to their ability. They received a physical examination and any laboratory procedures or X-rays required. There were a few beds set aside for those needing them. But the department's main thrust was to eliminate hospitalization except when it was absolutely necessary.

This was a milestone for the hospital, and it demonstrated its determination to keep pace with the always growing needs of the community. A report in November of 1956 showed just how great these needs of the community had grown. It showed that, during 1955, a total of 29,263 patients had been treated at Memorial—more than ever before in the hospital's history of 49 years.

Also in 1956, another one of the hospital's dreams became a reality: the School of Medical Technology. Because advances in medical technology were taking place at such a rapid pace, this was seen as an absolute necessity. Dr. Franz Leidler, Pathologist and Director of the Memorial Hospital Laboratory, became director of the new school. The program took up to ten students, who attended the school for 12 months, putting in an eight-hour-a-day schedule. At the end of the 12-month course of study, the students were qualified to take the national examination given by the Registry of Medical Technologists, and were then invited to join the American Society of Medical Technologists. It was a fully

90

accredited program, qualifying the graduates for a profession in that field, and, of course, a chance to continue their work at Memorial Hospital, if they so desired.

That same year Memorial established the Physical Therapy Department, with two full-time registered therapists, new emergency room equipment, and even new furniture for some of the patients' rooms. Air-conditioning was installed throughout the entire hospital, thereby eliminating another major problem.

One indication of the recognition the hospital was receiving, and of its commitment to quality medical education, was its official approval for a General Practice Residency (the only one in Houston), and a rotating internship.

The year 1956 was a very productive one in other areas also. The Ford Foundation granted Memorial Hospital $207,500 for "improvements or extension of hospital services to the community." Among the uses Memorial Hospital found for this generous donation were the renovation and modernization of the two oldest wings of the hospital; the enlargement of the X-ray Department, new laboratory equipment, the augmentation of facilities for the outpatient department, and the establishment of a physical therapy department. Also, a fourth diagnostic room was added to the X-ray Department.

The needs of the city could not have been better demonstrated than in the November 1957 announcement that the previous year set new patient records: 32,054. This was an increase over 1956 of almost 3,000 patients. With hard work and the help of the Ford Foundation grant, the hospital was able to keep pace with this growth.

In 1957, Mr. John Dudley was advanced to the post of Executive Director, from that of Hospital Administrator, which he had held for ten years. His Associate Administrator, Mr. W. Wilson Turner, was named Administrator. Together they took the hospital into the decade of the 1960's, providing the leadership needed to bring Memorial Hospital further into the forefront of innovation and change and establishing a path for other hospitals to follow.

The year 1957 also marked the Golden Anniversary for

Memorial Hospital. From the tiny 17-bed Ida J. Rudisill Sanitarium of 1907 on the corner of Smith and Lamar, the hospital had developed into a major facility by mid-century. The first growth period had occurred in 1911, with the addition of a four-story, fireproof building and basement which increased the number of beds to 50. In 1915, another enlargement added three more stories to the existing structure, bringing the total bed count to 100. By 1924, the hospital had once again reached its capacity, so a new wing was built, giving it 215 beds altogether. Another addition in 1942 brought the bed-capacity to 295, and in 1948, the opening of the seven-story Cullen Nurses Building was not only the realization of a dream for the Administrators, but completed a cycle in the hospital's history. It had now established itself as one of the most complete hospitals in Houston.

The next surge forward had come in 1952 when a nine-story brick addition known as "L side" was opened. Seven of the floors were entirely given over to patient areas, with the other floor containing 13 operating rooms. The beds now numbered 485, and by the year of the Golden Anniversary celebration, work had begun on a 15-story medical and professional building which would complete Memorial's expansion to two entire city bocks in downtown Houston.

A DOWNTOWN MEDICAL COMPLEX

Completed in the summer of 1958, the Memorial Professional Building was a milestone in the development of the Memorial Hospital System. This new building was grouped together with the hospital and the Cullen Nurses Building to create a medical facility unique to Houston at the time. Located across the street from the hospital, the professional building was linked to it by an underground tunnel. The physicians officing in the professional building could easily get to the hospital in the case of an emergency, or to visit their patients. They had at their disposal the most modern and advanced equipment and facilities possible, including the hospital itself. Each doctor had his own office, designed to his specific needs, and as an added convenience for both doctor and patient, a five-story parking garage offered safe, off-the-street parking.

The $5 million structure was also unique in design. According to Mr. Harold Calhoun, the architect for the project, the colorful exterior was expressive of the new culture of the Southwest. Designed of "curtain wall construction" (a system in which metal panels are placed on the structural steel beams), the garage was covered on three sides by an ornamental aluminum screen with red, yellow and blue porcelain panels. The portion of the building which contained the doctors' offices was constructed over the garage, and was covered with gold aluminum and vertical-pivoted windows. The design and vibrant colors of the building were quite different from any other structure in the city, and were the subject of much comment. But everyone agreed that the Memorial Professional Building, like the hospital system itself, was unique, and that once again Memorial Hospital had set a precedent, both in concept and design. In 1961, the Texas Society of Architects gave the building a Merit Award for excellence in design.

Architect Harold Calhoun, right; James Lyons, Assistant Hospital Administrator, left, and George Irving, Chairman of the Board of Trustees, with a model of the Memorial Professional Building.

Above, the Memorial Professional Building
under construction adjacent to the hospital;
Below, the finished product, completed in
1958.

Another field in which Memorial Hospital played a leadership role was Psychiatry. The hospital's psychiatric section was first organized back in 1941 by then Administrator, Mr. Robert Jolly, and Dr. Abe Hauser. It was the first in a Houston general hospital, and became one of the largest in the state of Texas. By the end of the 1950's, the unit had grown to 40 beds, and had the most modern forms of treatment available, as well as conducting research with new drugs. One example of how the hospital strived to offer the very best in patient care, was its employment of an Occupational Therapist full time to assist the psychiatrists in their practice. This form of therapy was just being recognized as a very vital adjunct to the treatment of emotional disturbances.

At Memorial, when a psychiatric patient was admitted, he was assigned to a private room, or to a bed in a small ward. In extreme cases, he would be given a bed in a special closed unit, where he would receive intensive care. Shortly after admittance, the therapist, having been advised of the patient's problems by the doctor, would visit the patient and encourage him to take part in the many activities and projects available in the recreation room.

The type of activities prescribed for the various patients were based on their emotional needs, according to the kind of expression required to help them adjust to their problems. For example, the patient who needed to express aggression or anger would be given a project that would call for physical actions to give vent to their emotions. Anything employing physical movement, such as woodworking or leather stamping, would achieve this goal. On the other hand, a patient requiring a tranquilizing activity would be assigned a form of needlework or something similar. A patient's background and interests were also taken into consideration when deciding on the form of treatment. Many painted, some tended plants, and some even undertook projects that were beneficial to the unit itself, such as repairing and painting the furniture, or making cushions for the chairs. When a number of patients enjoyed playing a small organ borrowed for a

Christmas party one year, the hospital started a fund to purchase an organ for the psychiatric unit.

Since the main principle of Occupational Therapy is to help the patient interact with others and learn to maintain satisfactory relationships, group association was an important part of the treatment. Several hours a day, the patients would work together at tables for six. The therapist stayed in the room with the patients and encouraged conversation with each other while working on the various projects. Realizing that personal appearance can have an effect on a person's mental well-being, Memorial even had a volunteer, who also was a professional beautician, come into the ward one day a week and give beauty treatments to those women desiring them. Obviously, the hospital did everything possible to assure the patients in the psychiatric unit the best care available under the most pleasant and near-normal conditions that a hospital situation could provide. In psychiatric, as in other areas of health care, Memorial Hospital maintained its position as a leader, not only in the city of Houston, but in the state as well.

In September of 1959, Memorial became the first hospital in Houston to have a course in psychiatry for physicians in practice. Although aimed primarily at physicians on the staff of Memorial Hospital, other practicing physicians could also apply. The National Institute of Mental Health of the U. S. Public Health Service gave a grant to the hospital to make this course possible, because it felt that it would fit in well with Memorial's educational programs. The goal of the program was to broaden the knowledge of physicians in treating problems of emotional origin. The teaching was conducted by psychiatrists from the faculty of the University of Texas Postgraduate School of Medicine. Physicians taking the course were encouraged to present cases from their own practice dealing with the problems of emotional disturbance. The objective of the psychiatry course, as stated in the Public Health Service Mental Health Training Grant, was "to meet the pressing need for clinically oriented and clinically competent personnel to assist in the recognition and care of persons with emotional and mental health problems, with a view to aiding the doctor in accepting a greater share of responsibility in the reduction and prevention of mental illness. The physicians will be trained in the psychological managment of the patient and to help the patient's family understand the illness and assist the patient." In keeping with Memorial's tradition of refusing to remain static in a rapidly changing world, it had now recognized and acted on the need of treating people for the problems caused by the stress of daily life in the Twentieth Century.

As Memorial Hospital approached the decade of the 1960's, it could look back at the preceding 53 years with pride, secure in the knowledge that it had, through sound administrative planning, taken its place as one of the leading medical facilities in the state. The progress and innovations which had occurred during the 1950's were particularly indicative of the sound structure of the past—and the bright promise of the future. By 1960, Memorial Hospital had become a total hospital, one dedicated not only to healing, but also to medical teaching and to the prevention of illness.

Lillie Jolly Class of 1957—The 50th Anniversary Graduation Class

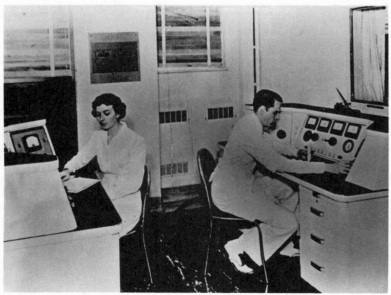

Top Photo: Memorial Hospital Medical Records Department in the 1950's; Bottom: X-ray Department in the 1950's

PERSONALITY PROFILE:
MR. JOHN G. DUDLEY

Mr. John G. Dudley was born in Fort Smith, Arkansas, and attended the University of Arkansas. He was the Administrator of the Baptist Hospital in Little Rock before coming to Memorial Hospital in 1946 as Administrator. In 1957, the Board of Trustees named him Executive Director of the hospital.

Mr. Dudley held many offices in state and national organizations during his years at Memorial. He served on the Board of Blue Cross and Blue Shield of Texas, on the Physicians-Hospital Relations Committee of the Texas Hospital Association, and as a member of the American Hospital Association. He was Vice Chairman of the Board for Texas State Hospitals and Special Schools; President of the American Protestant Hospital Association, President of the Texas Hospital Association, and a Fellow in American College of Hospital Administrators. He served as a Deacon of the South Main Baptist Church.

Mr. Dudley's accomplishments for Memorial were numerous. Among them were the addition of the 185-bed wing at the corner of Lamar and Louisiana; the unique Memorial Professional Building; the Southwest and Southeast Branch hospitals, and the over $5 million final addition to the downtown Central unit, which was under construction at the time of his death in 1963.

He instituted an internship for student pastors in chaplaincy work and secured full accreditation for the nursing school by the National League for Nursing. The American Protestant Hospital Chaplain's Association

A Memorable View of the Professional Building

PERSONALITY PROFILE
MR. JOHN G. DUDLEY
(Cont'd)

honored him with election as a Fellow of the Association "in recognition of his outstanding contributions in the field of hospital chaplaincy."

In 1964, the Baptist Hospital Association honored his memory with a special educational institute called the "John G. Dudley Memorial Institute for Trustees." His co-workers at the hospital characterize him as a man of dedication and sincere good will.

CHAPTER FIVE

"Creativity is a marvellous capacity to grasp two mutually distinct realities without going beyond the field of our own experience, and to draw a spark from their juxtaposition."

—MAX ERNST

MEMORIAL BECOMES A SYSTEM

Early in the 1960's, Memorial Hospital entered a new phase which could best be called "The Turner Years."

Mr. W. Wilson Turner had come to Memorial for the first time in 1947 as Assistant Administrator and served in that post until 1950. He returned to Memorial in 1955 as Associate Administrator and was made Administrator in 1958. His time as the man in charge of Memorial would span nearly two decades and would result in a totally transformed hospital. As Mr. B. J. Bradshaw, a prominent attorney and active member of the Board of Trustees, put it: "The emergence of Memorial Hospital as a prominent institution is due largely to the vision and the planning of Mr. Turner."

Some of the years of his leadership were tough times for hospitals generally, but Memorial not only survived, it flourished. The sixties and seventies saw Memorial retain and strengthen its position as a leader in city, state, and national health care. The steps to achieve this were many. They included first the expansion from a single hospital to a large multi-hospital system (one of the very first such organizations in the country). Then the hospital moved to establish a broader base in the Houston community. To do this it enlarged the Board of Trustees and dissolved its affiliation with the Baptist General Convention. After this came the movement of the hospital's Central unit from the original downtown location to the suburbs of Southwest Houston. This was followed by an innovative design for the main unit, a showcase for the newest and the best in general health care facilities. The new hospital also spurred crucial new developments in hospital financing for the state of Texas. Any one of these taken by itself would be a major administrative accomplishment. Taken together, they demonstrate how important The Turner Years have been in development of Memorial Hospital.

The first big change engineered by Mr. Turner came before he actually was in charge of the hospital, and it emerged as a creative response to the rapidly changing face of Houston. The United States Census measured the city's population in 1960 at 938,219, a huge leap over the 1940 figures of 384,514. Based on this growth, city planning engineers projected even greater growth for the next two decades; their estimates forecast what now seems a somewhat conservative figure, a population of over 2 million by 1980.

Memorial's growth had in some ways matched the city's own. Certainly by 1960 the hospital had become a very large institution. From the original wooden frame building and the eight nurses, it had grown into a hospital with 450 nurses, a total staff of over 1,000, and a net worth of close to $15 million. The sizeable staff and physical plant made it possible for Memorial to care for up to 446 patients, plus 60 babies, at any one time. It was possible for some 1,060 babies to be born each year in Memorial; for surgery to operate on some 52 patients a day, and for the emergency room to care for 32 patients each day. The total number of patients operated on per year had reached nearly 11,000. And these figures for direct hospital care tell only part of the story. The operation of a hospital this size required a kitchen staff of 138 workers, a maintenance staff of 41, and a cleaning staff of 116 people. There was even a laundry staff of 29 people who washed some 16,000 pounds of linens and uniforms every week.

THE CHANGING POPULATION PATTERNS

Large as Memorial was, however, Mr. Turner foresaw that the time was coming when the present home for Memorial would not be adequate to serve the city. The reason for this was the pattern of Houston's population explosion. Growth meant more than merely numbers; it also meant a new distribution of people. Houston, like so many large cities which experienced their periods of rapid growth in the automobile age, was expanding to the suburbs. People were settling far away from the location of the Memorial Baptist Hospital building on Louisiana Street in downtown Houston.

Mr. Turner's solution to this dilemma was, as we shall see, a complex, carefully thought-out plan, one whose innovations have been studied and imitated by many other hospitals across the country. The first stage of its presentation, however, echoes the spirit and the verve of earlier days in the hospital and the city. His answer to Memorial's dilemma was for the hospital to expand into a satellite system—to imitate, in fact, the department stores and other chain stores which had found a successful way to serve the new areas of population expansion.

For the proposed Memorial Baptist Hospital System, this idea translated into an arrangement whereby the system would build smaller branch institutions in the center of outlying suburban areas. The central hospital would be the main unit; it would provide special services to the smaller units, enabling them to upgrade patient care and at the same time enabling the institution to reach the whole city. The smaller units would also serve as feeder institutions to the main unit, sending it the patients whose cases needed special medical expertise or equipment. Thus, the plan was carefully worked out by Mr. Turner. Both the success of Memorial's system and the years of nationwide imitation have proved it sound.

All this skillful planning would not have mattered, however, if the idea had not been accepted and implemented. Mr. Turner's work to insure that this acceptance did come, suggests that his knowledge of human nature was as important an ingredient in Memorial's success as his knowledge of hospitals. Once the idea was developed in his own mind, he did not present it directly to the Board of Trustees. He relied, instead, on two things: curiosity and the inherent selling power of a good idea.

First, he drew up two huge, eight-foot by six-foot charts. One chart showed the current 1960 population and the other the projected population in 1980. These charts demonstrated the anticipated changes in distribution as well as in numbers of people, so that once the 1980 chart was superimposed over the 1960 chart, the suburban growth of Houston was featured clearly. This pattern demonstrated the need for a switch to the system structure. Once the charts were complete, however, Mr. Turner kept the plan quite literally under wraps. He put the large, eye-catching charts in a prominent place in his office, but he kept them covered. People could only wonder at their purpose and message.

The strategy worked perfectly. Mr. George Irving, then Chairman of the Board of Trustees, was frequently through Mr. Turner's office on his way to visit Mr. John Dudley, then Executive Director of Memorial. Mr. Turner's office was adjacent to Mr. Dudley's, so that each time Mr. Irving came to talk about the business of Memorial Hospital, he saw the outsized chart in Mr. Turner's office. When he asked Mr. Turner about it, however, the reply was carefully vague: "It's just a project I'm working on." Another visit and the same question resulted in a similar answer: "It's just a project I'm working on, and I don't think it would interest you much." More questions followed, of course. Finally, Mr. Turner did let it be known that it was a population study and that, yes, he did have some ideas on how the hospital might benefit from the shifts. Mr. Irving had to see it then, and, once he saw it he quickly realized how Houston would change and what the implications of these changes would be for Memorial Hospital. He soon "convinced" Mr. Turner that his idea for a satellite system was important and sound. The well-planned, extremely soft sell had worked. Mr. Irving advocated the plan to the Board of Trustees, and Memorial Hospital was soon on its way to becoming a system—one of the very first such hospital systems in the region and the nation.

On its way, yes. But the shift from excellent plan to achieved reality was not simple. The very size and complexity of the city which made the expansion plan so attractive also made it very difficult. Land was expensive. So were construction costs. And the amount of money available to the hospital was small. The hospital's affiliation with the Baptist Convention of Texas placed severe limitations on indebtedness, and also made difficult any community-wide fund raising efforts. A good plan for necessary expansion thus seemed stalled. This delay, however, ended with a stroke of good fortune.

A PROMISING DEVELOPMENT

As has happened so often in the history of Memorial Hospital, planning and ambitious goals for service were not allowed to simply fade away. Just when all seemed hopeless, a way to work out at least the first stage of the plan appeared. Mr. Turner, as he looked for a way to build the first Memorial satellite hospital in Southwest Houston, talked to the management of the Sharpstown Shopping Center about including a hospital as part of the center. The Sharpstown possibility did not develop, but it did lead to a meeting between Mr. Turner and a Houston builder and promoter named Mr. Stokes Adair.

It just happened that Mr. Adair was then in the process of building a hospital near the corner of Hillcroft and High Star Streets. The hospital was being built on a speculative basis; Mr. Stokes Adair hoped to sell the building on completion. After he and Mr. Turner talked, however, he agreed to an alternate plan. Memorial would lease the new hospital plant from him, thus guaranteeing an occupant for his new building and providing Memorial with the first of its new locations. With no money, Memorial had still gotten started on its plans to expand into a system.

This good deal soon got even better. Mr. Stokes Adair, pleased by the leasing arrangement which let him take rapid depreciation on the building, soon built another hospital on West Bellfort in southeast Houston. Memorial leased this one as well. Mr. Adair later built another hospital. This one, completed in 1966, was in northwest Houston, and Memorial leased it to complete the original satellite system. The idea which Mr. Turner had so carefully sold to Mr. Irving was now a reality.

This new system soon gained a degree of financial security as well. Mr. Stokes Adair, after he had taken the ten-year depreciation period on each hospital, gave his equity on each branch hospital to the system. Mr. and Mrs. Adair also furnished the chapels located in the Southwest and Southeast hospitals and donated an organ for each. The chapel at the Northwest Unit was furnished by the Baptist Temple Church and named the Jester Chapel, in memory of Dr. T. C. Jester, former pastor and also a former board member of the hospital. Memorial had, in a remarkably short time, moved from a one-unit hospital to a pioneer multi-hospital system. Yet in the midst of all the change, it kept its focus on service to the people of Houston, service which included attention to all aspects of the patient—spiritual as well as physical needs.

Exactly what the system operation added to the previous single Central Unit can be seen by a closer look at each of the branch hospitals:

The Southwest Hospital, which opened on June 4, 1962, was a 100-bed facility with sections for pediatrics, obstetrics, and surgery. The pediatric area had both an examining room and a playroom. The obstetrics section included four labor rooms, two delivery rooms and three nurseries—two of these were for newborn babies and one was for the treatment of sick infants. The surgical suite had four surgery rooms and four recovery beds. Each room had a private bath, and each room had modern furnishings including a television set. The hospital was completely air-conditioned. The hospital also had a radiology department, laboratory and blood bank, a pharmacy, and emergency rooms with an outpatient department. Parking space for 200 automobiles was provided.

Patient demand was even higher than anticipated, however, and exactly one year after the opening of this southwest branch of Memorial, construction began on a 25,000-square-foot addition. This two-story building was completed in six months at a cost of $500,000; in external design and room design it matched the original Southwest building and contained all the same amenities. The addition brought the total bed capacity of the Southwest branch to 165 beds.

Soon after completion of the addition to Southwest, the second satellite branch opened; Memorial Baptist Hospital Southeast was located at 7655 Bellfort Boulevard and opened on December 2, 1963. This hospital had 135 beds and, like its

Southwest Unit, Opened in 1962

Southeast Unit, Opened in 1963

counterpart in the southwest, was located near a freeway for easy access to the main hospital downtown. The Southeast hospital had 81 private rooms, 22 semiprivate rooms, and two five-bed wards. Each private room had a complete bath, television, telephone and modern furnishings. Semiprivate rooms had identical furnishings, bath and television. The hospital was completely air-conditioned with every room piped for oxygen. Rooms in the nursery, pediatric, obstetric, surgical and emergency rooms were piped with vacuum pipes for emergency suction. There was also parking space for 250 cars.

The obstetric section had four labor rooms, two delivery rooms and three nurseries. The surgery suite had six operating rooms and an eight-bed recovery room. The pediatric section included an examining room and play room. The Southeast branch at its opening also had a radiology department containing four diagnostic X-ray rooms and a radiologist on duty. It had a fully equipped pathology laboratory, including a blood bank, with a pathologist in charge, and a pharmacy with a registered pharmacist on duty. There were also emergency facilities with three treatment rooms. The hospital was staffed with regular staff physicians and nurses, and with interns, residents, student nurses and chaplain interns in the educational program of the hospital system.

So popular was the establishment of Memorial Southeast that some 6,000 visitors attended its open house on December 1, 1963. Southeast opened to patients the next day, and the first baby was born there on that day.

A SATELLITE FOR THE NORTHWEST

Plans for the northwest branch of Memorial were announced by Board Chairman Mr. L. D. Cain in 1963, and this facility, located at the North Loop and Ella Boulevard, was opened in 1966 with 130 beds. The Northwest satellite, like the first two, was constructed by Mr. Stokes Adair. The chapel here, furnished by the Baptist Temple Church, was

110

1966 Opening for the Northwest Branch

given in memory of longtime board member, Dr. T. C. Jester. The hospital had complete laboratory, X-ray, emergency, operating, and delivery facilities. It was air-conditioned and had parking space for 250 cars. Three years later, and just three years after the first coronary care unit was installed in Texas, a unit for coronary care opened at Memorial Northwest. This was part of Memorial's plan to install coronary care units in each branch.

A new addition to Northwest was opened in 1971. It brought the total number of beds to 220—making the Northwest branch the largest general hospital in the northwest area.

The innovative plan for a satellite system actually did more than take basic hospital facilities to the new suburban centers. It also divided duties between the branches and the Central unit in a way which enabled each to focus on certain aspects

of the health care delivery system. The Central unit continued
to serve the entire city and all types of patients. It also served as
the coordinating agency for all units in the system and took
care of such functions as:

> Conducting all educational programs for the
> entire system and assigning students to the
> branch units.
>
> Conducting research programs.
>
> Providing special services to patients not
> possible in most small hospitals.
>
> Performing certain functions such as
> purchasing, accounting, payroll, collections,
> laundry and so forth, for all units in the
> system.
>
> Assisting the smaller units in recruiting and
> training necessary specialized personnel.
>
> Providing supervisory services in all areas.

Each branch hospital was thus not completely independent
of the mother institution, but rather an extension of it. While
the branches served as feeder units—providing patients who
needed psychiatric or other very specialized care to the Central
unit—the total resources, including staff and equipment, of
that Central unit were available to the branches, enabling
them to operate at standards usually impractical for small
hospitals.

The branch hospitals, all located not more than 12 to 15
miles or not more than 20 minutes (at the time of the
founding) from the main unit, operated within an
administrative structure designed to take advantage of the
cost-saving possibilities inherent in the new plan: An
administrator, who actually was an assistant administrator in
the overall hospital system, was located at each branch and

was directly responsible to the administrator of the Central unit. All services which could be performed at the main unit without impairing patient care were done there in order to keep costs at a minimum. For example, the functions of accounting, payroll, laundry, purchasing and general stores were conducted entirely at the main unit.

The branch X-ray departments were prepared to do virtually all diagnostic procedures, but were not equipped with the costly machinery necessary to do X-ray therapy; Other services, such as laboratory work were divided. In the case of the laboratory, all "stat," or emergency procedures, were done at the branch, but main routine tests were actually carried out at the main hospital; Some of the other departments which, in effect, had substations at the branch hospitals were pharmacy and medical records. The facilities of the branch hospitals were used for teaching purposes much like the Central unit. Student nurses, chaplains, interns and residents were routed through both.

A VIABLE SYSTEM

The success of the total Memorial System plan, however, depended as much on the strength of the Central unit as it did on the creation of the new satellites; both were necessary if the hospital were to succeed. Thus, Mr. Turner, who had been named Executive Director after the death of Mr. John Dudley in September of 1963, oversaw the conclusion of an important addition to the downtown hospital. The planning had started during Mr. Dudley's term, and the construction of this nine-story, $6 million addition and enlargement project was finished in 1965.

The downtown addition enlarged the bed capacity of the Central unit to 600 and it also strengthened two other aspects of Memorial's health care tradition—its ability to use the latest medical technology and its capacity for health care with a personal touch. The new addition, for example, made possible the space to house a new $45,000 Cobalt Radioisotope Therapy machine. This new machine—one of a very few in the region—actually treated patient ailments. Whereas earlier X-ray machines could help a physician diagnose tuberculosis or a broken arm, the new cobalt machine could deliver a radiation beam which would destroy diseased tissue. Unlike other similar machines, this one could be easily rotated and maneuvered around the patient to reach malignant tumors deep within the body. The 1965 addition also provided a new public cafeteria and a newly remodeled "Peanuts Gallery" for pediatric patients; this room helped young children adjust to the hospital by featuring large blown-up copies of the famous *Peanuts* cartoon characters.

THE BOWLES CHAPEL

The Memorial Central unit also added a crucial element to the spiritual side of its healing ministry with the addition during this same period of the beautiful Bowles Chapel. This vital part of the complex, which was located on the corner of Louisiana and Lamar, had become a part of planning for the hospital as early as 1960. In the fall of that year, Mrs. William Victor Bowles and her daughter, Mrs. Fred T. Couper, Jr., had offered to make the hospital a gift of the chapel. They knew that Memorial wanted a place to house the spiritual phase of its ministry, and their offer of a chapel was accepted gratefully by the Board of Trustees. At that time the chapel was to be dedicated: "In loving memory of William Victor Bowles, by his wife, Edna Henderson Bowles, and their daughter." It was to be called the *William Victor Bowles Memorial Chapel*. Then in January of 1965, after a long illness, Mrs. Bowles died before the chapel could be completed. Mrs. Couper changed the name of the chapel to *The Bowles Chapel* and dedicated it to the honor of both her parents. The history is marked by two separate marble tables, the original for William Victor Bowles and a second: "In loving memory of Edna Henderson Bowles and William Victor Bowles by their daughter, Mary Frances Bowles Couper, Jr."

The chapel itself has been a continuous part of the Central unit since 1965. With the decision in 1969 to move the Central unit to a new location, the importance of the chapel to the hospital was underlined by the decision to move the Bowles Chapel, piece by piece, to serve as a key part of the new structure.

114

Altar view of Bowles Chapel

The design plans for the original chapel began in 1960 when Mrs. Bowles and her daughter discussed with Mr. Harold Calhoun, of the firm of Wirtz, Calhoun, Tungate and Jackson, their desire to have the chapel executed in the period of English Gothic Architecture. The choice proved to be an excellent one. Mr. Calhoun had a strong background in classical architecture, and he appreciated Mrs. Couper's strong interest in the project. He included her in all planning meetings.

After the first drawings were made to start implementing this suggestion, there followed four more years of research and planning to get the design exactly right. Since all of the planners felt that the project's success depended on the authentic design of all materials in the chapel—including the stone, woodwork, oak tracery, pews, chancel and vestibule furniture, chandeliers and hardware, and the marble floors— the research was painstakingly done. To insure faithful renditions of the early Fourteenth Century style chosen by the Bowles family and reproduced by the architects' design, much of the handcrafted work had to be done in Italy and England. All of the work had to be hand-crafted with great artistry.

As a result of the careful research, design, and craftsmanship, the Bowles Chapel can take those who enter its doors back into an age when ecclesiastical architecture was at its height. For those who need some solace or relief from the stress brought on by the illness of a friend or family member, the carefully wrought features of the chapel create an atmosphere of religious peace and comfort. The careful attention to authentic detail and to the creation of mood began with the beautiful Gothic doorway, made of white Italian Carrara marble, which is the outdoor entry to the chapel. This arch has been handsomely carved in the traditional ecclesiastical manner with oak leaf crockets and capitals. There is a cherub in the center of the arch and there are doves with folded wings on each side. Supported by the arch is a finely carved marble Cross Fleurie—the Cross decorated with flowers.

Through the heavy oak door of the entrance, one enters the

116

vestibule of the chapel. The walls here are of limestone with eight Gothic arches of carved stone, surmounted by stone medallions, and the ribs across the ceiling are finished in gold leaf. The floors of the vestibule area are of Bois-Jourdan marble of several colors in a diamond design. The same marble and the same pattern extend also to include the floors of the nave—the center aisle leading from the rear of the chapel to the chancel—and the side aisles. The inspirational beauty of the nave of the chapel is announced by a Gothic arched doorway of carved oak, surmounted by a Cross of oak. Inside, the soft color of the limestone walls forms a striking contrast to the rich dark tones of the oak tracery of the woodwork. The table for the altar is made from Italian Botticino marble and oak. Like the other furnishings in the chapel, it comes from Mrs. Couper's own extensive knowledge of antiques, her careful research, and her effort to find just the right piece of furniture. Above the altar table is the intricately carved reredos, an oak screen behind the altar. Within the reredos hangs the Dossal Screen of brilliant red silk damask, an English fabric, especially woven in Italy in Gothic design for the chapel.

Upon the altar itself stands an exceptionally rare and beautiful antique Cross dating from 1690, and four matching candlesticks. The altar set is made of carved wood and retains its original mellow paint and gilding. Two silver gilt flower vases, and a set of four matching candlesticks, complete the altar table arrangements. The seven beautiful stained glass windows follow the French influence of geometrical rather than symbolic design, which was characteristic of the Fourteenth Century. The hundreds of pieces of glass which went into the windows were hand-cut and polished, then hand-leaded.

The arched ceiling for the nave and chancel is of paneled oak, and from the ceiling hang four chandeliers, designed after a Gothic chandelier of the Fifteenth Century which still hangs in an English church. The candle arms of the chandeliers are festooned with oak leaves, with Gothic spires running through the center, and finished with eagle finials. Several of the lanterns hanging in the side-aisle and in the vestibule are antiques from an old English Priory. The other lanterns were all handcrafted in England especially for the Bowles Chapel, and were reproduced from the original ones. The oak pews are carved in Gothic design, and the cushions are upholstered in ruby red velvet. The hymnals, bound in red leather, were especially designed for the chapel. All of the doors are made from paneled oak, and the ornamental brass hardware recalls a Fourteenth Century design.

The parlor of the chapel is designed in the Jacobean style with paneled walls, beamed ceiling, and a stone fireplace. In the parlor are a number of fine antique pieces. A still-life painting by the Dutch master, Justus van Huysum the elder, hangs on one wall of the parlor. The painter, who was born in Amsterdam, Holland, in 1649 and died in 1716, was one of the Dutch painters who helped the art of flower painting reach its supremacy in the Dutch school. The painting depicts an open work brown wicker basket which has a profusion of newly picked summer flowers—roses, tulips, iris, and forget-me-nots—in the sunlight. Immediately behind these are large poppy leaves and in the background of the painting, van Huysum has placed an expansive background with trees.

Bowles Chapel Parlor

119

Mrs. Couper and Mrs. Bowles chose the painting because its tranquil beauty seemed appropriate to the chapel setting and because they wanted to insure that the chapel would always have flowers.

The rare Dutch chandelier in the parlor is made of "Latten," an early form of brass. The chandelier is inscribed with the name of the maker, the name of the church hall where it originally was placed, and the year in which it was made: 1639. It is believed to be one of the earliest dated chandeliers known. The small English "Lantern" clock is engraved with the name of the maker, the town of London, and the year it was made: 1659. The pair of Elizabethan andirons, circa 1600, are made of steel and brass. The furniture of the parlor is all antique, dating from 1660—1690. There is a small elaborately carved side piece known as an oak settle and called a "Court Cupboard." Two oak chairs upholstered in blue velvet are from the same period, and there are two tall cane-back William and Mary chairs. The carpet is an antique Tabriz Persian rug, dating from 1700. The dedication tablets located in the vestibule have been carved from polished Carrara marble with gold leaf lettering.

The Bowles Chapel gets regular use both for weekly religious services and special holiday services, for music recitals, and for wedding ceremonies. Its frequent use also by those who need quiet and comfort while they are at the hospital shows the importance of this special memorial section of the Central unit. Mrs. Couper herself says that "the rewards of the chapel are endless," and she counts herself lucky to have planned it. "There is," she says, "not a single thing I would change."

The completion of the chapel and the other additions to the downtown Central unit in 1965 also signaled the completion of Memorial Hospital's expansion into a true hospital system. That system itself has undergone some significant changes in the years since, but the innovative concept of the multi-hospital system has remained constant and has been widely implemented throughout the region and nation. It has been examined and praised in publications such as the *Texas Hospital Association Magazine* and the national journal, *The Modern Hospital.* Such studies show that the system concept has more than fulfilled its promise of improved health care to the Houston community. The public clearly benefits from the convenience of a health care delivery system which brings medical service to their suburban communities.

But the people of Houston also have benefited in ways which are, perhaps, not so immediately obvious. The centralized purchasing system, for example, has enabled Memorial to hold down the high costs of quality health care through combined purchases and combined administrative costs. As Mr. Turner noted in a 1966 article:

> *The cost of operating satellites is less than a completely independent hospital because they do not have comparable overhead expenses, many of which are borne by our Central unit. For example, the existing accounting department can absorb the accounting functions of the satellites at much less cost than establishing a new department in the satellite. The same is true for such areas as laundry, personnel department, purchasing, etc.*

The centralized laundry facilities not only avoid duplication of equipment but also allow for automation which would not be practical if the individual satellite operated on a completely independent basis. Even as early as 1966, the savings here alone were substantial. To do laundry at a typical hospital in that year cost 4½ cents per pound. But the shared resources of the Memorial system lowered that cost substantially to 3½ cents per pound. In itself, this penny-a-pound saving might not seem like much, but when multiplied by the volume of laundry done throughout the system, it is very significant. In 1966 alone, the hospital system was able to save some $3,000 per month by use of the combined facility. When savings in this one area are multiplied by other savings in other parts of the hospital, it is clear that the switch to a satellite system has brought substantial cost savings.

In fact, the benefits which have accrued to Memorial's

pioneer venture into a multi-hospital system have been increasingly imitated by hospitals across the nation. By 1975, there were some 370 multi-hospital systems in operation, and the number was increasing. Some 24 percent of all community hospitals and 32 percent of community hospital beds were part of systems. Memorial's successful early expansion help set a national trend which still continues.

PASTORAL CARE

Memorial's expansion to a system was the most critical development of the 1960's, but it was not the only one of importance. During this same time period, Memorial also added another crucial feature to its hospital services—the department of Pastoral Care. This department actually continued and extended the work of the chaplain's office, which had been installed shortly after World War II. Even before the office of chaplain was initiated, however, pastoral care can be said to have been an important part of Memorial's patient care. Mrs. Lee, the first hospital missionary, was succeeded by Miss Emma Musgrove. She was known to everyone connected with the hospital as "Miss Emma," and she had for many years offered religious comfort to Memorial patients. Although she never bore the official title of chaplain, she visited with patients and their families, passed out Bibles, and converted people to religion. So hard did she work, in fact, that one newspaper article written about her in 1942 listed her as responsible for 1,028 conversions and 2,016 reclamations during her years at the hospital.

The official chaplain's office, however, had its beginnings during Mr. Dudley's administration and with his appointment in 1948 of Chaplain Joe Fred Luck. Chaplain Luck was the first Protestant chaplain to be employed in a Houston hospital, and he served in that capacity for a number of years. During his period as chaplain, he wrote a monthly inspirational column for the Memorial newsletter, and he was active in the Chaplain's Association of the American Protestant Hospital Association. In 1959, he became another in the long line of Memorial employees to take on a national leadership role when he was elected President of the 500-member Chaplain's Association. This organization is designed to provide Protestant chaplains with the opportunity to exchange ideas, seek cooperation, and share information about their work; the election of Chaplain Luck to its presidency points out both the quality of the hospital's staff and its dedication to the role of the chaplain in health care.

By the 1960's, the hospital had two full-time chaplains, Joe Fred Luck and Kenneth Dial. These two men spent much of their time, of course, visiting patients, trying to see as many of them as possible. They also ministered to all hospital employees, and to all employees and students in the Lillie Jolly School of Nursing, with regular chapel services in the auditorium of the Cullen Nurses Building. In addition they held special services at Christmas and Easter, and they broadcast daily worship services—Scripture readings, prayer, and a short devotional meditation—over the hospital public address system for all patients who wished to listen. The heavy workload of these two men was supplemented by the help of what were called Chaplain interns. In a program planned by Mr. Dudley, these pastors or ministerial students gained clinical experience in the pastoral duties of visitation, counseling, and the conducting of worship, while taking parallel courses at the Institute of Religion in the Medical Center.

The affiliation with the Institute of Religion, in fact, brought Memorial the man who would eventually become its next chaplain. Mr. Tom Cole first came to work for Memorial Hospital in 1960 when he was a student at the Institute. He enrolled there after pastorates at churches in Covington, Kentucky, and McLean, Virginia, to carry out his goal of work in the field of pastoral care. Because he was a Baptist, Mr. Cole was assigned to Memorial for his internship. Then, just as he was finishing his studies at the Institute, Mr. Cole received calls from both Chaplain Luck and Mr. Turner; they wanted him to take a permanent position at Memorial. He accepted and the permanent position has turned into just exactly that; Chaplain Cole started full-time work in that year and still works full-time for Memorial Hospital.

Soon after he arrived, however, the need to further expand the services of the Chaplain's office led to some restructuring of the responsibilities there. Chaplain Luck was made assistant to Mr. Turner, the Executive Director of the Hospital; he assumed the responsibilities for arranging chapel services in all units of the hospital, for setting up visitation activities in all the units, and for representing the system in activities of the denomination. Chaplain Cole, meanwhile, was given the responsibility for heading up the Department of Pastoral Care and expanding the Memorial Program in Clinical Pastoral Education. That program, the first one in Houston, had begun with three students in 1954 and was now ready to expand both the number of students it could serve and the kinds of educational experience it offered. Today, the clinical Pastoral Education program continues to be strong in numbers and in the kind of experiences it offers in pastoral training.

The program seeks to prepare the ministerial student for the actual experience of pastoring. It is one part of a 50-year-old nationwide movement in Clinical Pastoral Education which seeks to supplement the standard seminary work of the Divinity student. Where the usual academic work at seminaries prepares the student for preaching and trains him or her in ethics, religious education, and the philosophy of ethics, the seminary usually (although more seminaries do this now than in the past) does not prepare the student adequately for the crucial interpersonal sides of the ministry—for the work of pastoring. At Memorial Hospital, the setting provides a very concentrated exposure to people undergoing crucial experiences of life such as birth, death and illness. In fact, it has been estimated that one year of work with hospital patients and their families who are under stress and who need guidance can provide the equivalent of ten years work in a more normal setting.

This compressed experience also has careful supervision and monitoring so that it serves as an educational experience as well. The educational program is what Chaplain Cole calls "an action/reflection model for learning ministry within a clinical environment." Each intern is assigned a unit of the hospital where he will serve as chaplain, so that a certain floor or pair of floors becomes, in effect, that Intern's parish. He

124

takes copious notes on the visits he makes, the conversations which he has with families, friends, and with the patients themselves. Later, these interviews and the notes on them are shared with the supervisor, and then the supervisor helps the intern learn from these encounters. The whole inductive process thus gives him concentrated practical experience *and* the opportunity to learn better pastoral skills through feedback about the experience.

The student also attends seminars which focus on issues similar to those dealt with during his internship work. The average full-time intern spends some 30 hours per week in patient visitation and in written assignments about his pastoral visits. The other ten hours of the week are spent in study seminars designed to add to the student's reading knowledge about the problems he faces each day.

This program, which began under the supervision of Chaplain Joe Luck in 1954, was the first such program in Houston. It began that year with three students, and it now has ten or more interns at a time in a program fully accredited by the Association for Clinical Pastoral Education. As these students improve their ability to communicate their faith, they also continue the Memorial Hospital tradition of ministering to the whole person—of caring about the spiritual and the emotional needs of the patient, as well as the physical ones.

The strong denominational history of the hospital can be seen in the interns who come from such places as the Southern Baptist Theological Seminary in Fort Worth, but there is also a diversity of educational background which represents Memorial's wish to serve all the citizens of Houston. In fact, the program in Clinical Pastoral Education has had students from every region of the country and from almost every faith group. The program—currently administered by Chaplain Tom Cole and staffed by two other full-time chaplains, Don Bratton and Tim P. van Duivendyk, who work as supervisors in the program—insures that all patients at Memorial will have access to spiritual care which is equal to the high-quality medical care provided by the Memorial medical staff.

There were also other significant educational developments at Memorial during the 1960's. The Central unit established the first hospital-based speech clinic in this part of the nation in a program which began in 1965. This venture teamed the resources of Memorial Hospital with those of the University of Houston to provide a program of training for audiologists.

Later in the decade, the Lillie Jolly School of Nursing and Houston Baptist University merged their curriculums to offer a baccalaureate program in nursing. The merger, which took place in 1968, had been studied for several years before that; a grant from the Houston Endowment made possible this plan to use the educational resources of the University and the clinical facilities of the Memorial Baptist System for complete education in nursing.

The changes which characterize this decade of the Memorial Hospital System and the city it serves were matched by equally important changes in the total structure of the health care industry in the country. In 1966, Congress passed the Medicare and Medicaid bills which provided federal financing for the health care of the elderly and the poor. Soon after this came a series of other federal laws which placed hospital employees under the minimum wage law. It was obvious that such changes would have massive and far-reaching effects on the health-care industry in the country. What was not so obvious, but still of crucial importance, were the effects of earlier legislation, the Hill-Burton Act. This program, which was designed to relieve the financial burdens of hospital construction, was just making its effects felt in the 1960's. This, plus the development of some large chains of proprietary hospitals in the 1950's, meant that in the 1960's there existed the unfamiliar possibility of too many hospital beds in the nation.

The possibility of too many beds was accompanied by another dilemma: the shortage of physicians in the country. These problems, coupled with the problem of inflation, would influence health-care costs. And, expectations for health care on the part of the American public were rising along with health care costs.

Science had begun to develop capabilities for preventative and restorative health care on a much larger scale than before. The hospital delivery systems in the country, however, were not designed to incorporate these changes easily. Memorial Hospital System, like other hospitals throughout the country, would have to adapt to meet these new conditions, and it soon became apparent that this adaptation would involve some major modifications in the traditional approaches to health care. Memorial, which through the years had survived and flourished by virtue of its successful adaptation to changes in the city and in the health care profession, would need even more adaptability and flexibility through the 1970's.

Among its traditions, however, Memorial had several resources which would help its continued success in the next decade. Houston knew and respected its long history of quality health care for the whole patient. Memorial had also the long tradition of excellent hospital administration as a resource. Mr. Turner, ready to lead the Memorial Hospital into the second decade of The Turner Years, was experienced and far-sighted, and he was constant in his devotion to the hospital. His ability both to envision the plans necessary for a great hospital and then to carry through on the complex steps necessary to embody those plans would be needed even more in the 1970's than in the 1960's.

His words on the eve of the hospital's expansion into a system form both the best summary of the hospital's spirit during the 1960's, and the attitude with which it entered the 1970's:

> *It is our sincere belief that Memorial Baptist Hospital possesses potentials of future growth and development unequaled by any other hospital in our area. We need only the wisdom and courage to launch out and take advantage of its opportunities in order to further develop it into a truly great institution of healing.*

Downtown Central Unit in 1963
(Memorial Professional Building at right)

Bowles Chapel Outside Entrance

PERSONALITY PROFILE:
MRS. MARY FRANCES BOWLES COUPER

Mrs. Mary Frances Bowles Couper, a member of the Memorial Hospital System Board of Trustees, and her mother, Mrs. William Victor Bowles, donated the Bowles Chapel to Memorial in 1960 when they heard about the need for a chapel at the then Memorial Baptist Hospital downtown. A beautiful and authentic replica of a Fourteenth Century chapel, the addition was originally planned for dedication to the memory of Mr. William Victor Bowles. After her mother's death, however, Mrs. Couper had the chapel dedicated to the memory of her mother and her father. When Memorial moved its main building in 1977, workmen painstakingly took apart the chapel and moved it piece-by-piece to its present location.

Mrs. Couper is a graduate of the Kinkaid School and attended the University of Texas at Austin where she is a member of the Fine Arts Advisory council of the University of Texas System. Mrs. Couper founded the Theta Charity Antique Show and has served as member of its board. She has also served on the Board of the Houston Speech and Hearing Center.

PERSONALITY PROFILE:
MR. W. WILSON TURNER

When President Emeritus of Memorial Hospital System Mr. W. Wilson Turner retired on May 31, 1981, he left behind a 30-year reputation for vision, careful planning, innovation, and concern for his fellow employees at Memorial. He also left behind a record of outstanding accomplishments for Memorial.

Mr. Turner graduated from Waco High School, and from Baylor University where his degree was in Business Administration. He also did graduate work in Business Administration at Northwestern University in Chicago. He worked as Office Manager for Hillcrest Hospital in Waco under the leadership of his preceptor, Mr. Lawrence Payne, before serving in World War II as the skipper of a mine sweeper in the Navy. After the war, he returned to Hillcrest Hospital in Waco until Mr. John Dudley offered him a job as Business Manager at Memorial. After three years, he was invited to become Administrator of the Baptist Hospital in Alexandria, Louisiana. From there he went to Mississippi Baptist Hospital in Jackson, Mississippi, as Administrator. Over these years, he and Mr. Dudley had kept in touch. Mr. Dudley always felt that Mr. Turner was really just 'on loan,' broadening his experience before returning to Houston and Memorial. In September 1955, Mr. Dudley called Mr. Turner back to Memorial where he has stayed.

His accomplishments during the next years were many. He pioneered the satellite hospital system at Memorial, a new way of cutting health care costs. This system began with the Southwest Unit in June 1962, followed soon after by the

Southeast Unit in 1963. Mr. Dudley died in 1963, and Mr. Turner followed in the footsteps of his good friend by becoming Executive Director. In 1965, the Central Unit downtown added a wing and the Northwest Unit also opened. In the late 1960's, Mr. Turner led Memorial in planning the innovative total health center at 7600 Beechnut. Like the satellite system, this building, with its use of automation and mechanization, has been widely studied in the hospital industry.

Mr. Turner's career has been marked by many professional offices and honors. He has been President of the Texas Hospital Association, President of the Texas Association of Hospital Accountants, President of the Houston Area Hospital Council, President of the Baptist Hospital Association, and Director of the Texas League for Nursing. He also served as a member of the Board of Directors of Blue Cross and Blue Shield of Texas, a member of the Council of Manpower and Education for the American Hospital Association, and a Fellow of the American College of Hospital Administrators. He has been an active member of the Willow Meadows Baptist Church, serving there as a Deacon and as its Chairman twice. He is now a member of the Second Baptist Church.

In 1974 Mr. Turner was honored with the prestigious Earl M. Collier Award for distinguished Hospital Administration. This award for integrity, competence, and leadership in the field of hospital administraion was presented to him at the Texas Hospital Association Convention in Dallas; it was accompanied by a standing ovation from his colleagues in the field.

In 1979 he was selected as the recipient of the American Protestant Hospital Association Award. This award is given annually for outstanding leadership and unusual contributions in the field of church-related health care. The award cited his accomplishments in creating the satellite system, in securing passage of state legislation in Texas to let hospitals take advantage of tax exempt bonds, and his development of the Memorial Hospital System Chaplaincy

Continued on Page 132

MR. TURNER
(Cont'd)

Program. In 1981 Mr. Turner received the Founder's Award from the Texas Association of Hospital Governing Boards for dynamic leadership in hospitals and the community.

Mr. R. William Warren, now President of the Memorial Hospital System, and a man who had Mr. Turner as his preceptor, praises him for the progress brought about by his vision and his leadership. He also praises him for another key aspect of his career: his personal commitment to Memorial's patients, medical staff and employees.

PERSONALITY PROFILE:
MR. F. M. LAW

Mr. Francis Marion Law worked his way up in the banking business, beginning as a bookkeeper and assistant cashier in Bryan, and then working as a cashier at the First National Bank of Beaumont before coming to Houston. He moved to this city in 1915 as a Vice-President of First National Bank; he became Senior Vice-President and then, in 1930, President of the bank. After World War II, he became Chairman of the Board. Throughout his career, he was active in state and national banking activities.

In 1924 Mr. Law was elected President of the Texas Bankers Association, and in 1933, President of the American Bankers Association. (Mr. William A. Kirkland, in his history of the First National Bank, characterizes him as "a forceful and entertaining speaker and a public-spirited citizen of the first rank.") He was a longtime Chairman of the Board of Directors for Texas A&M University. He served for 43 years on the Board of Directors at Memorial Hospital and was Treasurer of the Board from 1925 until 1963.

At that time, in honor of his 43 years of service on the Board and the many ways in which he contributed to the hospital's progress, the Board dedicated the new outpatient department of the downtown hospital to him. A plaque was placed in the lobby of the outpatient department with the inscription: "The Board of Trustees of Memorial Baptist Hospital, Houston, Texas, dedicates its outpatient department to Francis Marion Law for many years of faithful service. 1963."

PERSONALITY PROFILE:
MR. GEORGE M. IRVING

Mr. George M. Irving received a law degree from Baylor University and then returned to his home town of Palestine, Texas, to practice law. He came to Houston in 1927 at the invitation of a former courtroom opponent, A. B. Culberson, who was a bank officer at the Second National Bank of Houston. Mr. Irving joined the bank, now the Bank of the Southwest, as a Trust Solicitor. He was elected Vice President in 1942 and became a Director and General Trust Officer in 1947. He was also Chairman of the Board of Farnsworth Company, Vice President and Director of the Mainland Company of Texas City, and Director of the Sugar Bowl Gas Company, Sugar Bowl Utilities, Inc., and Sugar-Bowl Dehydrating, Inc.

He was very active in Baptist and civic affairs. He served as a Deacon at Second Baptist Church, as an active worker in the United Fund, and as a member of the Board and President of the Houston Heart Association. He was a member of the Baylor University Board and of the Board's Executive Committee for Baylor Medical School.

Mr. Irving served for 18 years on the Memorial Hospital Board of Trustees, and for ten years, from 1949 to 1959, as Board Chairman. Prior to his election as Chairman, he served as Chairman of the Building Committee during the construction of the Cullen Nurses' Building. Under his leadership as Board Chairman, the hospital had several major building programs, including the building of the Lamar-Louisiana wing which added 185 beds, and construction of the Memorial Professional Building and parking garage.

Continued on Page 135

PERSONALITY PROFILE:
MR. LESTER D. CAIN

Mr. Lester D. Cain served Memorial Hospital as a member of the Board of Trustees from 1951 until his death and as President of the Board of Trustees from 1959 to 1964. Prior to that he served as Vice-Chairman of the Board and as Building Chairman. With his help and leadership, Memorial Baptist Hospital became one of the most completely equipped and outstanding hospitals in the United States. He also led Memorial during its expansion into a system.

A native of Yoakum, he started to work in the oil fields around Goose Creek, Texas, and later became President and owner of the L. D. Cain Oil Company. Mr. Cain was a member of South Main Baptist Church where he served as a Deacon. He was a member of the Board of Trustees of Baylor University, Houston Baptist College, and the University of Corpus Christi. He also served on the Human Welfare Commission of the Baptist General Convention of Texas. Although he asked that his name not be mentioned at the time, Mr. Cain donated the first iron lung in the state to Memorial Hospital.

In recognition of his leadership and his gifts to the hospital, the name of the Board Room at the Central Unit was designated The Cain Board Room.

MR. IRVING (Cont'd)
In 1960 he was honored with a special scroll paying tribute to his years of "efficient and dedicated leadership" and his "unselfish service."

PERSONALITY PROFILE:
CHAPLAIN JOE FRED LUCK

Chaplain Joe Fred Luck graduated from Southwestern Baptist Theological Seminary in Fort Worth. He served as Chaplain with the 8th Air Force in Europe during World War II and as Chaplain of Arkansas State Tuberculosis Sanitarium in Booneville, Arkansas. He came to Memorial as Chaplain in 1948 as the first Protestant Chaplain to be employed in a Houston hospital.

In 1959, he was honored by election to the Presidency of the Chaplain's Association of the American Protestant Hospital Association. This national organization, which then had some 500 members, encourages Chaplains to attain the highest possible standard in their service and provides them with the opportunity to exchange ideas relative to their work.

During his years at Memorial, he helped plan, organize, and implement the program in Pastoral Education. He also conducted worship services for the hospital staff and for the nursing students, and visited as many of the patients as possible. He instituted a brief morning worship service which all patients who wished to hear could listen to over the intercom system.

In the early 1960's, the increased size of the hospital made it necessary for him to become Assistant to the Executive Director of the Hospital, Mr. Turner, and shortly thereafter, his duties were expanded to include the task of Director of Development.

CHAPTER SIX

". . . in the decisions we make now . . . the future is committed."

6

MAJOR CHANGES

The major changes which mark Memorial Hospital's history in the seventies were really set in motion by the Board of Trustees in the last part of the previous decade. At that time, the Board commissioned a study by the hospital consulting firm of Block, McGibony, and Associates, which was submitted to Mr. Turner on March 8, 1969, under the title "A Master Plan for the Memorial Baptist Hospital System."

The purpose of the study was to insure the "continued orderly growth of quality medical services," and it examined the hospital's service area and its areas of influence, the effects of recent and future hospital growth on the service area, the present and future need for hospital beds in the community, the adequacy of the existing hospital plant, and future requirements and needs of the hospital for fulfillment of its role in the community.

This lengthy and comprehensive master plan looked at a Houston downtown area which had changed greatly with the expansion of the city outward. Downtown Houston was still healthy, but its composition was different. The banks, oil companies, and related enterprises had kept their offices downtown, but other professional groups had moved away from the central city. In 1940, 70 percent of the doctors, 76 percent of the engineers, and 30 percent of the architects worked in the central business district. By 1963, only 14 percent of the doctors, 24 percent of the engineers, and 10 percent of the architects remained downtown.[2]

Parking, too, had become a problem; there was little room for Memorial's traditional patient base to find parking space, and the cost of new parking facilities was prohibitive. The downtown location also meant there was no room for

---

[2]See McComb, Chapter Five.

expansion to accommodate new facilities or provide space for needed new equipment.

The consultants' report addressed these and other related problems crucial to Memorial's future. In so doing, the study confirmed the feelings of the hospital's leadership and emphasized the need for a positive response to the situation. It was clear that the downtown Central unit, which had served the hospital well, now needed to be changed—that a new hospital needed to be built in a new location.

The solution, however, was not that simple. A new building meant a vast amount of money. To raise such a sum would require basic changes in the way that the hospital structured itself and its relation to the community. Such changes were necessary for two reasons. One was that the Baptist General Convention of Texas, with which the hospital had close ties, was morally opposed to accepting government funds for capital expansion; the Convention did not want any institution affiliated with it to accept such funds. The second reason was equally important: the Baptist Convention specified that only Baptists could serve as board members. It was obvious to the Board of Trustees, to the hospital administration, and to the outside analysts, that if the Memorial System was to continue serving the growing and diverse Houston community, the Board of Trustees needed broader community representation. The need for change thus was clear.

This brought up for careful consideration the hospital's long-term ties to the Baptist General Convention—a Baptist heritage which had served both the Convention and the Memorial Baptist Hospital System well. Tradition and continued growth were at odds with each other, and it was clear that any decision would be a difficult one. The Board of Trustees did vote, however, to request release from Convention control. This plan was presented to the Executive Board of the Convention, which referred it directly to the Convention without recommendation. The reasons for this decision by the Trustees, and for the eventual supporting vote by the Convention, are perhaps best summarized in parts of a speech which Mr. Turner made to the Union Baptist Association Annual Meeting on Monday, Oct. 11, 1971:

The present mortgaged indebtedness of the hospital is $15,054,000, representing a mortgage debt to total assets ratio of over 40 percent. Annual debt service payments, including principal and interest, total $1,622,000. This places the hospital at a very serious disadvantage when compared with other local competitive institutions which have constructed their facilities with the help of governmental funds.

The Hospital is now effectively controlled, as are other hospitals, by very strict governmental regulations and standards. Policies are presently dominated by the federal government. Over 30 percent of our patients are Medicare patients whose bills are paid by government. These governmental payments cover services on the basis of "allowable costs" only—certain expenses plus depreciation based on historical costs. This reimbursement is insufficient to cover capital requirements, since capital funds are available from other governmental sources through grants or subsidized loans which are unavailable to us as a Baptist institution.

Last year we were required to give the government discounts totalling in excess of $1,225,000 on their patients, indicating reimbursement substantially less than the true cost of delivering the service.

He went on to explain that it had become "imperative that a new major facility be constructed as soon as possible to serve as a base hospital in our system, replacing in this capacity our present Central unit."

Addressing the problem of how to finance the new facility, Mr. Turner went on to say that such financing needed "substantial support from the community through a major fund-raising effort, as well as support available to us in the

141

form of grants and/or subsidized loans through governmental sources." If the proposed facility was to become a reality, he said, "major financial support from non-Baptists is essential."

These facts, which were so strongly supportive of a break with the Baptist convention, did not however obscure the still important spiritual dimensions of the hospital's work, which had been there since its 1907 founding. In this speech, and in later presentations to the Convention, Mr. Turner emphasized that this link would be protected:

> Memorial is recognized throughout the nation for the excellence of its pastoral care educational program. We are very proud of this program and it is our desire to continue a close working relationship with the Baptist General Convention of Texas through contractual relationships for its chaplain, pastoral care and other appropriate affiliations.

When the Texas Baptist Convention met in Houston in October of that year, the proposed separation of Memorial from the Convention was a major issue. The messengers to the Convention voted 1,466 to 724 to uphold the policy of the Convention against the acceptance of federal aid, thus protecting church-state separation. There was heated debate on this issue, with those in favor of aid acceptance arguing that the aid would be reimbursement for services incurred by federal programs like Medicare. This proposal had the support of a report prepared by a special study committee of the Human Welfare Commission of the Convention. The Human Welfare Commission report also offered a recommendation that hospitals like Memorial be released from the Convention, with close ties maintained through a chaplaincy program.

This second recommendation, which supported Memorial's plan, met with better success. After discussion, the vote was taken and the result was an overwhelming 907 to 353 decision to release the hospital from its Convention ties. One crucial step in the movement toward a new main unit had been taken.

The momentous and necessary decision did leave some bitterness, however. There were some who felt that the Convention was giving away sizeable assets which belonged to it. One member of this group even filed an injunction to have the separation procedure halted. This attempt was short-lived, however; in view of the convention vote and the actual financial contributions which the convention had made to the hospital, District Judge William Holland of the 127th District refused to approve the injunction. After appearances by Mr. Turner; Mr. Vernon G. Garrett, then Chairman of the Board of Trustees; and by Dr. James Basden, secretary of the Convention's Human Welfare Commission, the plaintiff's attempts to show prejudice on the part of convention officials failed. During the hearing, Mr. B. J. Bradshaw—lawyer for the firm of Fulbright and Jaworski, member of the Memorial Board of Trustees, chief defense counsel for the hospital—made the crucial point that the Houston hospital system was not owned by the Convention. He argued, instead, that the hospitals were under the overall management of a nonprofit corporation. In the hearing process, Mr. Bradshaw also questioned Mr. Turner and Mr. Garrett in order to demonstrate the relative smallness of the budget contributions made by the Convention. Out of the more than $20 million operating budget for 1970 and 1971, contributions from the Convention were less than $175,000 each year. The hearing lasted only two days, and the temporary injunction was dismissed.

A NEW NAME—A NEW STRUCTURE

After the vote and a short delay due to the hearing, the word "Baptist" was deleted and the name was officially changed to Memorial Hospital System. The enlargement of the Board of Trustees to include more non-Baptists and more representation from the business expertise available in the city was helped by the existence of an Advisory Board. This

143

adjunct to the regular Board had been formed earlier in anticipation of the changes. Since its 20 members had already been at work advising the Board and working with it on the issues involved in long range planning, the change-over to a new structure was made rather quickly. The enlarged Board of Trustees structure was in place by January 1, 1972.

The new Board had a great deal of material with which to work. Memorial now had a 65-year history of leadership in health care in Houston and the nation. It had a seasoned administration, an excellent medical staff, and a large number of supporters in the Houston community. It also was planning an $80 million health care facility—a new main unit to replace the downtown Central unit. The land for this, recently purchased from Houston Baptist University, was a 38½-acre tract in the suburbs of the Southwest where Houston was moving. This property, which was bordered by Beechnut and the Southwest Freeway, would help continue Memorial's plans—first voiced with the satellite system proposed by Mr. Turner in the late 1950's—to take quality health care to the centers of Houston's population.

In arguing for the release of Memorial Hospital from the Convention, Dr. E. H. Westmoreland, Pastor of Houston's South Main Baptist Church and a Memorial Trustee from 1938 until 1960, had urged the Convention messengers with these words:

> *If the Memorial Baptist Hospital System is to survive as a first-class hospital—and one of the top non-governmental hospitals in the country—then we must release it.*

The release had been enacted, and Memorial now had most of the elements in place for another move forward.

One crucial element, however, was not yet in place: money. The total cost of the new hospital project would be $70,802,000—to be raised from a combination of sources including hospital operations, bank construction loans, sale of the land for the old Central unit downtown, and a capital fund drive. The bank loans would later be

144

supplanted by permanent financing from Equitable Life Assurance Co. and Teacher's Insurance and Annuity Co., and finally — after much work to set up a tax-exempt hospital bond program in Texas—by tax-exempt bonds for hospital financing. Part of the land downtown was sold to Gerald Hines Interests and is now the home of First International Bank Plaza. The other part was sold to Kenneth Schwitzer and is the site for the new Allied Bank Plaza.

The capital fund drive was conducted by a fund-raising team headed by Mr. Jackson C. Hinds. Mr. Hinds had become Chairman of the Board at the conclusion of Mr. Vernon Garrett's term, but Mr. Kenneth Montague took over the chairmanship to enable Mr. Hinds to chair the capital fund campaign. Mr. Hinds accepted the campaign chairmanship with the following announcement:

> *I think all of us feel a real sense of personal commitment to make health care better for all people. The medical complex which Memorial is planning will make a notable contribution to that goal and may well provide a prototype for hospitals of the future.*

Mr. Hinds was assisted in his work by the following members of the Steering Committee: B. J. Bradshaw, Paul R. Cole, Jerry E. Finger, L. E. Frazier, Jr., Vernon G. Garrett, Jr., F. O'Neil Griffin, Roy Huffington, Franz Leidler, M.D., Kline McGee, Kenneth Montague, S. I. Morris, Maurice Thomason, M.D., and Bernard Weingarten.

In addition, the following Houstonians guided the campaign activities as members of the advisory committee: Rex G. Baker, Jr., John R. Butler, James Elkins, Jr., Aaron J. Farfel, Earl C. Hankamer, Mrs. Oveta Culp Hobby, Ben F. Love, Edward J. Mosher, Al Parker, Eddy C. Scurlock, Carl B. Sherman, Milton R. Underwood, Dr. E. H. Westmoreland, Mrs. Gail Whitcomb, and Benjamin N. Woodson.

The capital fund drive began with a $1 million grant from the Houston Endowment, Inc. The Endowment is a nonprofit, philanthropic organization incorporated in 1937 by Mr. and Mrs. Jesse H. Jones to support charitable, educational, and religious activities in the city. Announcement of the gift was made by J. Howard Creekmore, President of the Foundation, and by Mr. Hinds. The grant, from a source well known to Houstonians as a source of funding for both cultural and health-service organizations, did much to get the campaign off to a successful start.

Further community support was generated by a visit to Houston by Dr. Louis Block, the consultant who had worked with the hospital on plans for the new facility. At a briefing report for the Houston media and the Houston public, Dr. Block mentioned his work in helping design more than 300 hospitals and stated that, "Memorial has planned the most comprehensive flexible facility anywhere in the country." Dr. Block also stated that: "When the new health care complex opens, the System will be ten years ahead of its time: it will be a prototype for the future."

As the capital campaign developed, gifts came from the M.D. Anderson Foundation, the Brown Foundation, the Clayton Fund, Exxon, the Shell Companies Foundation, Inc., Tenneco, and others. Before its conclusion, the fund drive successfully raised $7.5 million for the new hospital building. Gifts to help reach this total also came from Trustees, from large and small donations throughout the Houston community, from the Memorial Medical Staff, and from hospital employees.

WORKING FOR NEW LEGISLATION

At the same time that this public effort to raise money was being conducted, a somewhat quieter, but equally important, project was also going forward. This was the work to get tax exempt bonds for hospital financing in Texas.

The process for changing Texas law was arduous and time-consuming, but the results made it one of the most important aspects of hospital development in the state during the 1970's. Once the work was done, hospitals across the state, as well as Memorial, would benefit. The crucial bill to set this up had support from the Texas Hospital Association and from other

146

hospitals, but the major burden for the bill was carried by Memorial Hospital, its attorneys and administration. They first brought forth the proposal in 1973 under the sponsorship of Senator Jack Ogg. The bill did clear the Senate, but it got stalled in the House in an end-of-the-term calendar rush and did not pass.

During the two-year wait before it could be tried again, Memorial looked for other possible ways to find funding support for the new building; none of them worked. Mr. John Orr, bond attorney for Fulbright and Jaworski, brought the bill back in 1975 at the next legislative session. This time he and Mr. Turner were determined that the bill would pass. Mr. Orr recalls that they practically lived in Austin, making numerous trips there to testify about the proposal in formal hearings and to visit legislators to explain its benefits. The bill got past the Senate and then past the tough hurdle of placement on the House calendar by the House Calendar Committee. Here it ran into a potential problem: some legislators felt that only public entities such as schools and bridges should receive this financing help. After discussion, the bill did pass, however.

SUPREME COURT RULING

The long effort for tax-exempt hospital funding was still not over. Even after the bill had passed, there was a perceived Constitutional problem with the bill; to some people, it seemed to be an example of what is called a "conduit" financing maneuver, a plan whereby a nonprofit organization issues bonds for a third party. The procedures from here on involved complex legal moves within the mechanisms of Texas law, but essentially it was necessary for the Texas Supreme Court to hear such a case. An attempt in 1976 failed, but, finally, in 1977, Valley Baptist Hospital badly needed a building and tax-exempt financing. The Court heard the case, and it passed.

Memorial by now had financing in place from the Equitable Life Assurance Company and Teacher's Annuity. But both Hermann Hospital and Memorial Hospital decided to pay off loans for recent building projects and then to

147

refinance them through the new regional agency which grew out of the new law—the Southeast Texas Hospital Authority. Nearly a decade of planning and dedicated work finally yielded lower tax-exempt financing for the new hospital project.

It is appropriate that the long series of major events which had begun with Memorial's recognition that it must free itself from the Texas Baptist Convention would be concluded with the total health care complex—a structure which fulfilled the faith of Dr. Hermond Westmoreland and other supporters. It is appropriate, too, that the new possibility for tax-exempt financing, brought about by the persistence of Mr. Turner and Memorial, should benefit other hospitals as well. Memorial, long a leader in health-care innovation, had worked a change which would help other hospitals in the state update their own health-care delivery systems. In 1980, Mr. Turner was awarded the prestigious Founder's Award by the Texas Association of Hospital Governing Boards, in part for this work on hospital financing.

FAMILY PRACTICE RESIDENCY

The break with the Baptist Convention and the construction of a new facility were not the only important developments in the 1970's. On July 1, 1975, the Memorial Hospital System, in conjunction with the University of Texas Medical School at Houston, officially opened a new Family Practice residency program. The importance of this step can be seen by a brief look backward at the development of medical education in this century.

For the first half of the century, the focus was clearly, almost exclusively, on more and more specialization in medicine. The move was away from the horse-and-buggy physician who made house calls and who automatically saw his patients in a family context for all their ailments. In place of this was an emphasis on increasingly narrower and narrower specializations. But too often the new gains in medical knowledge which did come from increased specialization were not successfully applied, because that

148

same specialization so limited the ways in which physicians worked with their patients.

The American Medical Association noted this trend and started in 1969 to reverse it. That was the year that Family Practice was officially established as a medical specialty with new and comprehensive residency requirements.

Soon after this, the American Board of Family Practice was organized; it set both certification requirements and the educational means to achieve them. At the time that this Family Practice specialty was being organized, the Memorial Hospital System offered one of only 22 approved general practice residencies in the country. Since this residency was already part of the system, and since Memorial continued its strong interest both in medical education and in medical treatment for the whole person, the development of a *Memorial Hospital System Family Practice Center* was a logical next step. Planning for the program began in 1970 and culminated five years later with the opening of the center. The educational goal was not to overlook the knowledge gained, but to develop doctors whose knowledge and interests were broad in scope. With this breadth, the doctors would have the knowledge and the diagnostic skill necessary to know when to consult a specialist or refer a patient to one.

In 1972, the Family Practice residency program which would open in 1975 was officially established. Dr. Jack Haley, former Chairman of the Committee on Medical Education at Memorial Hospital, was appointed Chairman of the Division of Family Practice at the University of Texas Medical School.

The Memorial Hospital System/University of Texas residency plan sought, and received approval for, a total of 24 family practice residents—eight in each of the three years of its program. In addition to their primary work at Memorial in the Family Practice Center and in the hospital, the residents could rotate through M.D. Anderson Hospital, Hermann, St. Joseph, and the University of Texas Student Health Center. Today, under the Memorial Hospital/University of Texas program, both the university faculty and the hospital staff contribute to medical education.

Dr. Harold Pruessner became the first full-time

faculty/staff member of the Family Practice Center in 1972. In 1974, Dr. C. Frank Webber was appointed Director of Medical Education with a part-time faculty appointment at the University of Texas Medical School. He became Department Chairman and Professor of Family Medicine in 1977.

Members of the Memorial Hospital System staff who accepted appointments as academic chiefs were Ronald P. Mahoney, M.D., Internal Medicine; Henry B. Holle, M.D., Surgery; William H. Mack, M.D., Pediatrics; Robert H. Barr, M.D., Obstetrics; Robert Hauser, M.D., Psychiatry; Denny Harris, M.D., Anesthesiology; Robert B. Elliott, M.D., Orthopedics; DeWitt W. Cox, Jr., M.D., Radiology; H. E. Maddox, III, M.D., ENT; Jack N. Bevil, M.D., Emergency; and Franz Leidler, M.D., Pathology.

The Family Practice Program was aided by a four-year federally funded educational grant totaling $804,157. This grant helped underwrite resident stipends, purchase equipment and supplies, enable residents to attend medical meetings, provide faculty stipends, and finance a study of programs in Family Practice around the country. By the time the grant was awarded, such Family Practice residency programs numbered 200. Memorial's program, built on its base of the longtime general practice residency, was one of the most successful in the country. When it opened in 1975, there were over 100 applications for the eight residency positions open. With the program in place and with the move to the new hospital facilities, its attractiveness has grown even stronger. Today, due largely to the Memorial Program, some 25 percent of the graduating medical students from University of Texas Medical School choose Family Practice for their residencies.

Three special features of the way in which the Memorial Program in Family Practice has developed deserve notice. One of these is the model Family Practice office. First opened in 1975 with the center, this "model office" idea was added to the residency program requirements in order to give the resident some practical experience in how to set up and organize a private family practice office. By introducing them early to the problems involved in setting up and running an office, the program prepares them for better actual patient care when they leave.

A second and distinctive feature of the Memorial Family Practice program is the annual Norma Culmer Award. This award has a history which reflects many of the qualities found in Memorial's history. The late Norma Culmer, R.N., was the first nurse employed in the Family Practice Center in February of 1975. She learned that she was terminally ill in 1977, but made the brave decision to continue work despite her illness. Her friends recall her willingness, kindness, and understanding, and the award in her name honors a recipient for similar dedication as a resident in the Family Practice Center.

Recently another award has been established: The Harold T. Pruessner, M.D., Award which was inspired by Dr. Pruessner's excellence in teaching at the Family Practice Center. This award honors the outstanding senior resident.

OTHER DEVELOPMENTS OF THE DECADE

This progress in physician education in the mid 1970's was followed later in the decade by yet another educational innovation. Although it is too soon to tell, there are indications that this new program may prove as important in its own way as the Family Practice program. Memorial's new School of Community Health Education seeks to teach the value and the means of better health maintenance to patients. John Sims, Project Coordinator, explains that the purpose of the school is "to provide a foundation of health information by which intelligent decisions can be made." Courses, taught by professionals in the field, cover such topics as Emergency Medicine at Home, Nutrition through the Life Cycle, and Coping with Stress. Once again, Memorial finds itself in an area where there are few models to imitate. But, where the usual practice for hospital educational programs has been to offer just a few courses on an occasional basis, Memorial does plan a full range of offerings. Since the three pilot courses were swamped by applicants, and since both student and instructor evaluations requested that the first courses be repeated and additional ones offered, there could be a very bright future for this new kind of patient education venture.

During the same period, the last class from the Lillie Jolly School of Nursing was graduated in 1970 and the curriculum merger with Houston Baptist University was completed.

The first health screening service in the state was also opened by the System during this period. After a year and one-half of planning by a special committee from the medical staff and the administration, Memorial put into practice its plan for augmenting a patient's usual physical examination and offering the physician a variety of health measurements at a modest cost. Patients referred to the center by their personal physician could have a wide variety of tests including hearing testing, electrocardiogram, chest X-ray, visual acuity, glaucoma screening, pulmonary function evaluation, urology, urinalysis, hematology, blood pressure and chemical profile.

Also in 1971, the Northwest branch opened a new wing which brought its total number of beds to 220 and which made it the largest general hospital in the northwest area of Houston. The new addition was designed for use by Coronary Care, Intensive Care, Pediatrics, and surgical patients. The Southeast Unit also announced plans to expand its facilities to keep pace with the increase in patient demand. The addition added two floors of patient rooms and 70 beds.

The system underwent several major organizational changes during this period, and the effect of these changes was the modeling of Memorial more and more along the lines used by business corporations. The Board abolished the office of Executive Director and changed Mr. Turner's title to President of the System.

In May of 1971, Mr. Turner was installed as President of the Texas Hospital Association. His inaugural address on that occasion dealt with problems facing hospitals, and the benefits which could come to them from statewide cooperation. One part of this inaugural address had special application to his own hospital base at Memorial. Quoting Daniel Bell, he said: "The world of the year 2000 has already arrived. For in decisions we make now, in the way we design our environment, the future is committed."

These remarks might well have been addressed to one of the

crucial projects then being carried out at Memorial: the design of the new building. While on the one hand, fund-raising plans and activities were being developed, on the other, Mr. Turner and his associates from the Board, the medical staff and the administration were working very hard on the problems—and the possibilities—of building design. Their work with the architectural consultants of Block and McGibony and their own architect, S. I. Morris Associates, sought a hospital plan which would embody new concepts for a more efficient, more cost-effective hospital environment.

A TRADITION OF INNOVATION

They started with a certain, quietly revolutionary assumption of hospital health care and design. Simply put, they envisioned an environment *suited for the person as a patient*. Hospital rooms too often merely replicated the bedroom at home without taking into account the fact that once a person became a patient, room requirements were likely to be more sophisticated and more complex. They also wanted an environment that could accommodate change or growth, especially changes related to advancements in medical technology. Too often in hospital construction the structural life of the building is far longer than the technological life of the building—the period during which it can incorporate new technological aids. The planning group desired a structure which would prevent technological obsolescence and which would enable the technological life of the building to match its structural life. Such a design would reflect the changing and dynamic nature of the Memorial Hospital System.

What the planners came up with as the answer to all of these challenges is the current Memorial Hospital building at Southwest Freeway and Beechnut. When the large, new structure was financed, and finally opened in 1977, it embodied new concepts of design in all aspects of the building—from the individual patient's room to the shape of the overall structure. The success of the long planning efforts can be measured not only in the positive response of individual patients, but also in the response to the building by those who come from all over this country and from abroad to see and study its creative approach to the problems of hospital design.

The innovative room structure can be seen in the document on Page 157, copied from the original architectural proposal. The plans, however, only provided an abstraction. Mr. Turner recalls that before the hospital agreed to them, extensive and practical testing was done at the hospital itself. A model room in the unusual shape shown in the diagram was set up and actually used by the medical staff and the nurses. Out of this came the design which the architects, S. I. Morris Associates, felt would have the flexibility for growth and for adaptability within the structure.

The arrangement of these room units into clusters, and into floors, was also unique. The 10-bed cluster concept has many advantages when compared to the hospital corridor of conventional design. It provides flexibility, the capability for the internal manipulation and restructuring of space and—crucial to Memorial's emphasis on quality patient care—it also provided for minimal circulation of traffic throughout the floor. This, in turn, holds down noise and other external distractions for the patient. When combined into a hospital floor as shown in the illustration, the center of the floor then provides space for support services. The total service area then provides one section of the building spine, from which the cluster units radiate outward, forming the unique Memorial snowflake configuration.

These basic principles of the design were then fit into a total plan with other features to aid patient comfort and medical efficiency. The hospital floors, for example, are linked to the floors of the professional building next door by enclosed walkways which make it easier for doctor and patient to consult with each other.

Another important innovation for the new building was its extensive network of communications. The heart of this multi-phase plan is the patient communication system, which has allowed two major improvements over standard systems: more efficient filling of patient requests and less interruptions for nursing personnel. This was accomplished

154

without any major change in what the patient does in calling for service, but once that call is placed it is received by a central console operator. This operator quickly determines what the patient needs and then employs the staff locator function. What this means is that all nurses and nurse assistants carry a small radio transmitter only slightly larger than a ball-point pen. Each category of personnel has a transmitter which gives a slightly different radio signal, so that the operator simply calls up a specific floor and locates the nearest person in the category needed to help the patient. Thus, the nurses do not have to receive every patient request, all of which do not involve them, and they can be told of the patient's needs without having to go through the time-consuming walk to a central location and then back to the patient area. Like the hospital room design, this innovation was carefully tested in actual practice as the new building was being planned.

Another communication feature for the new building was the complex system of pneumatic tubes designed to keep staff members in the operating areas from having to interrupt procedures and leave for supplies. Some 30 stations located throughout the hospital can transmit hospital items through a large—four inches in diameter—cylinder which moves through a pneumatic tube. The carriers can go both ways in this system, which was designed to handle items ranging from pharmaceuticals, to medical records and X-rays, to computer printouts, and even small surgical instruments. This tube network and the patient-call system are supplemented by an extensive in-house intercom system—a Centrex phone system which allows patients to have direct dial-in-and-out facilities and also allows for consultations or mini-conference calls among employees on their own phone sets; and by an extensive in-house public address system.

One other aspect of the design for the new Memorial hospital building which deserves special mention is the computerized Physician's Registry and room-and-bed-status report. This sophisticated information system was made possible by the hospital's computer base system. It stores information on each patient admitted to Memorial and then

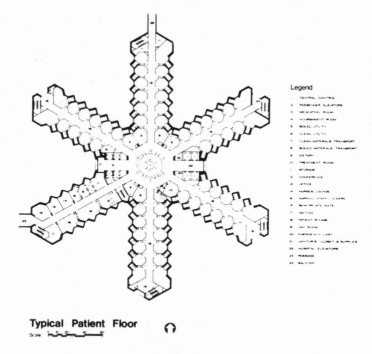

Legend

1. CENTRAL CONTROL
2. PASSENGER ELEVATORS
3. MEDICATION ROOM
4. NOURISHMENT ROOM
5. SOILED UTILITY
6. CLEAN UTILITY
7. CLEAN MATERIALS TRANSPORT
8. SOILED MATERIALS TRANSPORT
9. DIETARY
10. TREATMENT ROOM
11. STORAGE
12. CONFERENCE
13. OFFICE
14. NURSES LOUNGE
15. NURSING STAFF LOCKERS
16. SEMI-PRIVATE SUITE
17. WAITING
18. PATIENT ROOMS
19. DAY ROOM
20. EMERGENCY CART
21. JANITOR'S CLOSET & SUPPLIES
22. HOSPITAL ELEVATORS
23. PASSAGE
24. BALCONY

Typical Patient Floor
Scale 0 10 20 40 80

THE MEMORIAL "SNOWFLAKE" CONFIGURATION

A Planning Session for the New Building

156

THE NEW MEMORIAL HOSPITAL

A Model of the Unique Room Design

updates that material with information from each department which serves the patient. That information, or selected parts of it, can then be made available to departments or to physicians who need it. When, for example, a physician checks into the hospital, he can be provided with all necessary and updated information about his patients, including a variety of notices about conditions or changes which need his attention. The room-and-bed-status report uses virtually the same information, except that the material is printed out by patient floor. This not only provides basic information on patient location and status, but gives the admitting office and nurses timely information about bed availability.

What all the sophisticated communications network meant to the planners of the new building can be summed up in one phrase: more personal medical care at a lower cost. The substantial time savings in paperwork would mean less money and hours spent that way, and more medical staff and nurse time for working with the patients.

Another crucial feature of the planning for the new facility was the application of advanced technology to some of the other aspects of "everyday" hospital operations.

One major innovation was in the transportation of supplies within the building. The hospital was designed to save time by the use of electronically guided carts to transport supplies. A signal cable embedded in the floor guides a battery-operated vehicle which transports the cargo carts to predesignated points. So sophisticated is the system that each vehicle can call an elevator, proceed to a specific floor, and then discharge its cargo at the desired destination. This system greatly reduces the number of personnel required for transport work, without sacrificing efficiency or safety. It delivers food, supplies and linen throughout the hospital; then returns discarded supplies, soiled linen and soiled dishes to a central reprocessing facility where the components of the system are washed and sterilized. A recent article about this system in *The Dallas Times Herald* notes that it is the only one of its kind in a Texas hospital, and one of the biggest in North America.

One more crucial service area which makes use of automation to cut costs and provide better patient service is that of food preparation. Here, conventional home food preparation methods are used to assure that the food is appealing and of high quality; then modularized processing units are used to cook, package and chill the food in bulk and single-portion sizes. This automated process streamlines storage and distribution. The time saved here for the large number of patients, employees and visitors at Memorial is substantial. If the food preparation system were not automated, it would take 15 hours per day and seven days a week for this task. The automated system, however, requires only eight hours a day for five days a week.

A PLAN WITH A PURPOSE

This comprehensive planning for the new hospital building was a demanding and a time-consuming task. It promised, however, to work even further improvements in providing quality medical care at low cost.

Under the Satellite system, Memorial had successfully reduced the national average of 2.71 employees for each patient to only 2.18 employees per patient to deliver health care that was at once highly effective and highly personal. The same determination and skill on the part of Memorial administrators, trustees, and staff went into planning the new medical complex. When Mr. Turner and Mr. Garrett presided at the ground-breaking ceremonies for the new building in March, 1974 (see Page 167), it was clear that the new building would be a worthy addition to Memorial's 67-year tradition of innovative care for the people of Houston.

The new hospital was opened formally on January 30, 1977, with a ribbon-cutting ceremony involving Houston Mayor Fred Hofheinz; General Chairman of the Memorial Hospital campaign, Mr. Jackson C. Hinds; and Memorial President W. Wilson Turner (see Page 167). Although the weather was cold and wet, several thousand people attended the opening and toured the new facility, guided by employees. Behind the scenes of all this formality, however, had been a massive moving process.

The problems involved in transporting two separate hospital units—the original Southwest unit and the large Downtown facility—were, as an article in *The Houston Post* described it, "mind-boggling." It took months of planning to make sure that everything from furnishings and bulky equipment—to delicate surgical instruments and patients— could be moved. Mr. Kenneth Blankenship, Director of Memorial's Management Engineering said: "There were 25,000 major furniture and equipment items, and 75,000 separate boxes of goods to be moved from Central and Southwest." Yet the planning paid off and the mammoth move went smoothly. Even one particularly hard-to-move patient finally was satisfactorily settled into the new location. The man, the last patient to leave Southwest after all patients had already been moved from both of the other units, had been in traction for over a month after an automobile accident. Since he could not be moved either by car or by conventional ambulance service, the move of man and traction equipment was finally done by moving van. In an effort covered by local radio and television stations, he made it to the new hospital without a hitch.

Another item requiring special care in the move was the Bowles Chapel. Though it is hard to imagine when one looks at the quiet beauty of the chapel now, the entire structure was dismantled and then moved from the old location at the corner of Louisiana and Lamar to its new home on the northwest side of the new hospital.

Mrs. Couper was concerned when she heard about the plans to move the chapel; its fragility seemed to be no match for the rigors of moving men and vans. The actual move, however, went surprisingly well. Mr. James P. Miller, the Building and Construction Manager for Memorial, supervised the moving job, which employed eight full-time people for eight months, at a cost of $220,000. The men first crated and stored the furnishings, then took out the wood and the stonework piece-by-piece. The only difficulty was with the floor; the special marble imported for the floors had so many soft veins that it broke badly. The rest of the

"Moving Day" Scenes

Final Touches to lettering for new Bowles Chapel Sign

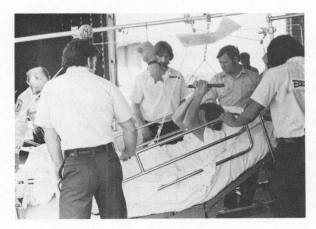

Traction and all —Bekins may never never forget this

161

complicated process went so smoothly, however, that Mr. Miller said: "If I had it to do again, I'd do it the same way. It went back in too perfectly to say I'd change anything." Mrs. Couper was also pleased with how well the valuable antiques of the chapel were preserved throughout the move; she said, "It's absolutely astonishing to me how they did it." The broken marble floors were replaced with similar stone, and the Bowles Chapel, an especially cherished part of the old Central unit, was preserved.

While the new complex was being planned, financed, and built through the early 1970's, other important developments were occurring in the Memorial System. The hospital was, for example, keeping up with the rapid advance in medical technology which continued throughout the decade. This included new equipment such as a fetal monitor (to monitor fetal heartbeat during labor), a unique set of X-ray equipment known as the C-arm image intensifier (capable of taking pictures and simultaneously transmitting them for rapid diagnosis over a television monitor), a maximal exercise stress lab (for the detection of coronary-artery problems before they occur) and a second special X-ray (for comprehensive and detailed radiography). The acquisition of machines such as these was crucial for any large hospital which wished to remain at the front of health care service. What made them doubly significant at Memorial is that many of these machines were purchased by funds provided largely through the efforts of the Memorial Auxiliary.

VOLUNTEERS-AN ADDED DIMENSION

The Auxiliary had been a part of Memorial from the first. In fact, the original founders first established a nursing school and then as their second act formed the Women's Auxiliary. They raised money from Houston churches, and as the years went by, from other churches in Texas, and administered a Love Fund to help poor patients and to fund nursing scholarships. They also performed services for the sanitarium at Auxiliary meetings in the homes of the members, where they made jelly and rolled bandages for patients.

The Volunteer Service organization, however, was first

organized in June 1948, when 12 women met at the First Baptist Church. The group was called the Junior Auxiliary, with Mrs. W. J. Baum as the President. They immediately launched several projects under the direction and leadership of Mrs. Robert Jolly. The first of these was a "Bookmobile" service for patients. The volunteers took donated books and magazines from room-to-room throughout the hospital twice a week, and gave them to patients. They also worked to promote the school of nursing by providing entertainment and parties for the student nurses and by establishing scholarships for them. As the number of volunteers increased, so did the services offered. Soon the Bookmobile circulated through the hospital every day and volunteers also helped staff the Information Desk at the main lobby.

Then, under the leadership of administrator John G. Dudley, who saw the great potential inherent in volunteer services, a full-time Volunteer Director was employed. This took place in 1953. At the same time, the original senior Auxiliary of the hospital and the volunteer organization—the Junior Auxiliary—were combined into the very successful Volunteer Services.

A few years later, in 1957, another important change took place: a group of girls between 15 and 20 years of age was organized into the "Candy Stripers." This carefully screened group of girls was given orientation and on-the-job training. This part of the organization proved useful in two different ways; the good will and cheer of the young women helped the patients and also many of them decided to pursue a career in health care. Some ten girls from the first group, for example, entered nurses training.

The woman who organized both the Candy Stripers and the Gift Shop, which opened later in the early 1970's, was Mrs. Ella Mae Bowers. She came to Memorial as the Director of Volunteers on a temporary basis and stayed for 17 years. She had been a volunteer at Memorial for some six years before taking the Director's job, so she knew firsthand about the potential for good in the organization. She and Administrator, Mr. John Dudley, worked together to expand greatly the volunteer organization and services.

Today, "The Caring Team," as the MHS Volunteer

Organization calls itself, is—like the hospital itself—a large and complex organization. Individuals join the Memorial Hospital Auxiliary and choose to donate their time to either the Memorial Unit, the Southeast Unit or the Northwest Unit. Each hospital group then elects its own Unit Board, which includes a Chief Executive Officer, a Director of Volunteers, and a number of individual committee chairmen who choose projects and set policies for their units. There is also a System Board which encompasses all three units. This Board includes on its membership the Chief Executive Officer of each Unit Board, the three Directors of Volunteer Service, two members at large from each unit, and officers who are elected at large by the volunteers. The System Board establishes policies applicable to all units, awards scholarships to nursing students, and disburses funds. The funds collected by the System are expended on projects which benefit the entire system.

A DISCIPLINED COMMITMENT

The people who make up this Volunteer Services network are as diverse as the city they serve. They include men and women from teenagers to those in their 80's. They are retired people and they are people who are fully-employed but still manage to devote some time to others. All of them, however, are committed to help and care for those around them, for a specific amount of time each week. And all of them also undergo training provided by a veteran Caring Team member, in orientation classes. These classes reinforce the idea that volunteer work requires serious and disciplined commitment. They also learn their roles as people who help supplement patient care, and as helpers to the hospital staff, as well as what it means to be a health care professional who performs in an ethical and confidential manner.

Once the general orientation is over, the volunteer receives training for a special job of his or her choice within the hospital. This job today can range from helping to prepare patient areas, to taking care of excess clerical work, to helping in the recovery rooms, to assisting new patients through the rigors of admitting.

Each of the units also offers unique opportunities for volunteers to become involved in special projects. At the Memorial Unit, for example, the volunteers conduct an indepth O.B. Tour for expectant parents. The people who enter the program see a slide presentation, tour the labor room, the nursery, and patient rooms, Then, they have a question-and-answer session with a knowledgeable volunteer. Volunteers at Southeast provide current magazines, recorded on records and cassettes in Spanish and English. These "talking books" are brought to the rooms of those patients who are physically and visually impaired. The Northwest Unit furnishes volunteers in pre-surgery to comfort patients before they go into the operating room.

Volunteers contribute to the individual units in other ways too. Since June 1971, when the first gift shop was opened at the Central Unit, volunteers have performed gift ship jobs at Memorial as regular business enterprises. The volunteers involved go on buying trips, keep inventories, and watch their inventories just as if the shop were their own. The profits which come from each hospital's gift shops then provide the funding to redecorate parts of that individual hospital and to purchase new medical equipment.

The most important contributions of the volunteers cannot be measured in money or even in hours worked. The helping hand, the smile, the sympathetic ear and the word of encouragement which they give to Memorial patients could not be bought. They are a crucial link in continuing Memorial's tradition of caring. The volunteers also provide a new perspective for the Hospital. As Joyce Robinette, Director of Volunteers, has noted, "The hospital is committed to the community, and volunteers are a part of both that commitment and of the community." The view which they give, then, is like the services they provide—unique and irreplaceable.

The Memorial Hospital System moved toward the end of the decade not only with outstanding community support from its many volunteers, but also with a strong group of loyal employees. Their dedication could be measured by the large number who each year received pins commemorating 5, 10, 15, 20, 25 and even 30 years of service in a wide range of positions at the Hospital. There was even one 45-year service pin presented to Miss Marie Burgin, Administrative Assistant of the System and a 50-year pin given to Pete Gonzales (see photo). When Mr. Kenneth Montague, Chairman of the Board of Trustees, presented service pins in 1982, he noted that the employees being honored represented almost 2,000 total years of service, and that "it is you, its employees, who make it the great institution it is today."

By the end of the 1970's, Memorial could look back with pride on the way it had responded to the events of the past ten years. The major challenges to quality health care had necessitated major changes, not only in Memorial's formal relationship with the Texas Baptist General Convention, but also in its own governing structure and its location. The Memorial Hospital System had met the challenges well, however, and these changes had enabled it both to strengthen its place as a leader in innovative health care and to increase its ability to bring quality health care to the still growing city of Houston.

Mr. Turner, rounding out nearly two decades of leadership at Memorial, received two awards which attest not only to the quality of leadership during his years, but also to the strength of the institution he led. He received in 1979 an award from the American Protestant Hospital Association for outstanding leadership in the field of church-related health care. In 1980, the Texas Association of Hospital Governing Boards named him as recipient of their Founder's award, for dynamic leadership in hospitals and the community.

Above: Groundbreaking for the new Memorial Hospital at Southwest Freeway and Beechnut in 1974, with Vernon G. Garrett, Jr., at microphone. Below: Ribbon-Cutting in 1977, with Mr. W. Wilson Turner and Houston Mayor Fred Hofheinz presiding.

The prestigious Earl
M. Collier Award

Vernon G. Garret,
Jr., discussing new
hospital

Pete Gonzales, left, recipient of a 50-year service pin, entered Memorial Hospital in 1917 as a patient and stayed to become one of its most valuable orderlies.

Kenneth Montague, Chairman of The Board of Trustees, giving out service pins

170

PERSONALITY PROFILE:
E. FREEMAN ROBBINS, M.D.

Dr. E. Freeman Robbins graduated from Baylor Medical School in Dallas and first reported to the medical staff of the Baptist Sanitarium in Houston in 1911. He chose surgery as his medical specialty because "it offered the greatest hope medicine could hold for the ill." His duties also included helping with clinic patients, opening the pharmacy and lab, and riding on emergency calls (in a horse-drawn ambulance). For these responsibilities, he received a salary of $10 a month.

In an interview in 1973, when he was 84 years old, he commented on the progress of the medical field. Early in the century, he saw hospitals begin to change from a home for the sick to a more active involvement in defeating disease and promoting health. He also noted the dramatic advances in medicine after World War II, especially in medical technology, pharmaceuticals, and advances in diagnostic, therapeutic and surgical techniques. What pleased him most at that time, however, was a return to some of the older emphasis of treating the whole person: "I'm so pleased to see family practice become a recognized specialty —it's a return to some of the best things of early medicine. We had specialists in the early days, but it was not until after World War I that they began to limit their practice to their specialty. Until that time, even specialists treated the whole man, and usually the whole family."

Dr. Robbins was Memorial's first intern, and it is appropriate that he became well-known in the city for his dedication to people. When he closed his practice, it included the children and the grandchildren of his first patients.

PERSONALITY PROFILE:
MR. R. WILLIAM WARREN

Mr. R. William Warren began work at Memorial as an Administrative Resident under the preceptorship of W. Wilson Turner on July 1, 1963. He graduated from the University of Texas with a degree in Sociology, and then completed the academic work for an M.B.A. in Hospital Administration at George Washington University, before coming to take the final required one year of residency work at Memorial.

One longtime member of the hospital who remembers this time recalls that "he was a real ball of fire even then. . . Whatever he was asked to do, he did yesterday—the best Administrative Resident ever to come through here." It was fortunate for the hospital, then, that he came to Memorial after completion of his degree.

He started work at Memorial as Administrative Assistant, then the Assistant Executive Director for the hospital. Although his thesis study of the effect that changing to a multi-hospital system has on the medical staff indicates his knowledge about the medical staff area of hospital operations, his background prepares him to know about the employee side of things as well.

This ability to understand firsthand many of the complex tasks which make up today's hospital has already been put to good use during his term as President of Memorial. As Memorial, and the health profession in general, faced a severe nursing shortage, he learned about the problem personally by meetings with over 75 groups of nurses, to hear their views of their profession.

Mr. Warren's first major administrative post at Memorial came not long after completion of his degree when he was appointed as Administrator of the Southeast Unit. He remained in that post until 1965 when he was named the System's Director of Finance. He then was named Assistant Executive Director and in 1971 was made Senior Vice-President. In 1978, he assumed the title Executive Vice-President of Memorial Hospital System. On November 1,

1980, the Board of Trustees named Mr. Warren President of the Memorial Hospital System.

He has been active in many professional and community organizations; is past President of the Houston Area Hospital Association, the Texas Association of Hospital Accountants, the Texas Hospital Information Systems Society (Distinguished Member); and has served as Chairman of the Council on Administrative Practice of THA. He has served on or chaired numerous association committees. He currently serves on the Board of the Texas Hospital Association as Treasurer and on the Board of the Voluntary Hospitals of America; is an Alternate Delegate from Texas to the American Hospital Association, and is Chairman of the Texas Voluntary Cost Review Committee for the Texas Voluntary Effort.

Mr. Warren has contributed to many industry publications, has presented numerous papers to professional groups in the state and across the nation, and is an active speaker on health care subjects.

PERSONALITY PROFILE:
MR. JACKSON C. HINDS

Mr. Jackson C. Hinds received his M.B.A. from Harvard Graduate School of Business in 1947 and his L.L.B. Degree from the University of Texas in 1948. He held various posts for Houston Natural Gas Corporation and its subsidiary companies prior to being named Executive Vice President and Director of the corporation in 1967. Later in 1967, he was named President of United Gas. He is now Chairman of the Board for Entex.

Mr. Hinds is also extremely active in civic affairs; he has served as President of the Houston Housing Development Corporation, Chairman of the Mayor's Advisory Committee on Housing, and Director of Main Bank, Houston. He also has served as a Director of Medical Center Bank, University Savings Association, the Houston Symphony Society, the Houston Chamber of Commerce, and the South Texas Chamber of Commerce.

He has been a member of Memorial Hospital's Board of Trustees since it was reorganized in the early 1970's and was appointed Chairman of the Board of Trustees in 1972. Soon after that, however, he agreed to become Chairman of the Fund Drive for the new hospital building, and resigned as Board Chairman in order to serve in the new post.

PERSONALITY PROFILE:
MR. L. E. FRAZIER, JR.

Mr. L. E. Frazier, Jr., is a Houston attorney and a partner in the law firm of Andrews, Kurth, Campbell and Jones. Mr. Frazier graduated from Baylor University with an A.B. Degree and received his L.L.B. from the University of Texas, where he was a member of the scholastic legal fraternity, Phi Delta Phi. He served as a dive bomber pilot in the Navy for four years during World War II. Mr. Frazier has served as Deacon and as Chairman of the Board at River Oaks Baptist Church. He has also been active in scout work and has served on the Board of Trustees of the South Texas Children's Home.

Mr. Frazier has been a member of the Memorial Hospital Board of Trustees since 1963, and served as its Chairman from 1965 to 1968. As a member of the Board, he was instrumental in the development of the satellite system, and also helped develop affiliation agreements with Houston Baptist College and with the University of Texas for medical education. He was instrumental in the restructuring and broadening of the Board of Trustees in the early 1970's.

In 1973, his dedication to Memorial Hospital and his accomplishments on its behalf were recognized when he won the prestigious Founders Award given by the Texas Association of Hospital Governing Boards, an organization designed to assist all agencies interested in maintaining and elevating the standards of health care institutions in Texas. The Founders Award honored Mr. Frazier for his leadership and his distinguished contributions to health care.

PERSONALITY PROFILE:
MR. KENNETH E. MONTAGUE

Mr. Kenneth E. Montague was born in Beaumont, Texas, and received a B.S. degree in Geological Engineering from Texas A&M. He entered the oil business in 1938 as a geologist for Standard Oil of Venezuela, then served with the U.S. Navy from 1942 to 1946. He worked for Sun Oil Company from 1946 until 1965. In February of 1965, he was elected President of General Crude Oil Company.

When General Crude merged into a subsidiary of International Paper Company in 1975, Mr. Montague was elected Executive Vice-President for Minerals and a Director of International Paper, in addition to his position as President of General Crude. In 1980, he resigned those positions and became Vice-Chairman of the Board at Entex. He was Chairman of the Board of Mid-Continent Oil and Gas Association from 1973 to 1975, and President of Texas Mid-Continent Oil and Gas Association from 1969 to 1971. He has also served as a director and a member of special committees for such organizations as the American Petroleum Institute; the National Petroleum Council; the American Institute of Mining, Metallurgical and Petroleum Engineers, and the Independent Petroleum Association of America. He has been a member of the Board of Trustees of the Texas A&M University Development Foundation for several years, and served as Chairman of the Board in 1975.

Mr. Montague joined the Memorial Hospital Board of Trustees at the time of its reorganization in 1971, and has

Continued on Page 178

PERSONALITY PROFILE:
MR. VERNON G. GARRETT, JR.

Mr. Vernon G. Garrett, Jr., was born in Carthage, Texas, and graduated from Baylor University in 1947 with a major in accounting. After serving with the Navy Air Corps, he came to work for the Houston Office of the Arthur Andersen Company. He is an audit partner for that firm, where he has been employed for 35 years. During those years, he has been a very active civic and church leader. He is a Deacon of the South Main Baptist Church, and has served as Chairman of the Deacons and of the church finance committee.

Mr. Garrett has been a member of the Board of Trustees for Baylor University, and has served as the President of the Baylor Alumni Association.

He has also given time and leadership to local and state hospitals and hospital associations. He has been President and Director of the Texas Association of Hospital Governing Boards and is a member of the Council of Allied Hospital Associations. He also serves on a Visitation Committee for M. D. Anderson Hospital patients.

As a longtime member and past Chairman of the Board of Trustees of the Memorial Hospital System, Mr. Garrett has been instrumental in the progress of the hospital in recent decades. He brings to that service not only his financial knowledge and background, but also a rare warmth and ability to work well with people.

MR. KENNETH E. MONTAGUE
(Cont'd)

served as Chairman of the Board since 1973. During his period of leadership at Memorial, the hospital has planned, financed, and moved into its new building, completely revised its corporate structure, and continued its expansion by building ties to hospitals such as Polly Ryon Memorial Hospital of Richmond.

CHAPTER SEVEN

Productivity is the issue for the Eighties. . .

MEMORIAL ENTERS THE 1980's

In 1979, as the Memorial Hospital System began to look back over its accomplishments in recent decades and forward to the new challenges of the 1980's, Mr. Kenneth Montague, Chairman of the Board of Trustees, and Mr. Wilson Turner, President of the System, issued a joint statement listing what they saw as the major issues facing hospitals. These, presented in terms of expectations, included:

- Expectation by the public that more services will be provided;

- Expectation by the medical profession that facilities will keep pace with technology;

- Expectation by all Americans that our health care system will be unsurpassed in quality anywhere in the world;

- Expectation by the Federal Government that these demands will be met within cost limits that were set with only limited regard for the factors which influenced cost.

None of these problems, stated in the annual report of the hospital, are new ones; they have been part of American health care concerns for the last few decades. Very similar pressures led Memorial to move to the satellite system in the 1960's and on to the major changes of the 1970's. What has happened, however, is that the various and often contradictory pressures generated by these expectations have become stronger over the years. As public expectations—and Houston's population—continue to increase, the hospitals of the area will have to find more and better ways to handle the needs, and the opportunities, of the 1980's.

Memorial Hospital System occupies an enviable position in this effort. As a pioneer in the cost-effective satellite system, it has a firm base on which to expand the basic plan of shared management and shared services. One way in which it has done this is through its affiliation agreements with other hospitals in the region. The precise nature of each affiliation is flexible and changes to meet the particular needs of the affiliates; the end goal of improved medical services through increased efficiency remains constant.

BIRTH OF THE COOPERATIVE PLAN

The Memorial System has also applied essentially this same technique in another direction. As it has joined other institutions to its system, it has also joined this system to a larger one by becoming a founding member of a very large hospital cooperative. This cooperative, called the Voluntary Hospitals of America, Inc., was founded in 1981. Somewhat like the Memorial Hospital System on a larger scale, this large hospital group uses its size to reduce purchasing costs, improve management effectiveness, and provide special services.

Another prominent asset as Memorial enters the 1980's is its even longer tradition of continuity in management. When Mr. W. Wilson Turner took over the top management position at Memorial after the untimely death of Mr. Dudley in 1963, he was already well-trained in hospital management and well acquainted with the specific problems and the possibilities at Memorial Hospital. When Mr. Turner then retired to the post of President Emeritus in 1981, his successor, Mr. R. William Warren, had almost 20 years of administrative experience at the hospital. This long line of careful training and stability at the top means that the Memorial Hospital System has now, as in the recent past, a unique leadership resource in its administration.

A similar stability can be seen in the number of devoted Board Members who have been active in hospital work for Memorial over many years. Trustees like B. J. Bradshaw,

182

Vernon G. Garrett, Jr., Kenneth E. Montague, and L. E. Frazier, Jr., not only bring the special knowledge of their own professions to the Board, they also bring with them a knowledge of Houston and of Memorial's own history and structure.

Memorial's stability does not mean stasis, however. The 1980's at Memorial offer new areas of emphasis and new directions. Some of these stem from its size. Memorial, for example, is now one of the largest providers of health care to the people of Harris County. Although some other medical institutions in the state also serve large numbers of patients, many of their patients come from outside the area and outside the country. With its three large hospitals in Houston, its ten affilated institutions in the surrounding areas, its over 1 million square feet of space, and its over 3,500 employees, Memorial has become a very large health-care business and one of the largest employers in the city of Houston

FOCUSING ON PRODUCTIVITY

Although any institution this size would have to be interested in employee productivity, this is especially true of Memorial Hospital, where about one-half of the $88 million gross revenue goes for employee salaries. Personnel costs have always been a major part of any health care expense, and Memorial has always tried to plan and work efficiently. For the 1980's, however, System President William Warren has designed a specific program to emphasize this goal.

In a special meeting early in his administration, Mr. Warren named productivity as the issue for the 1980's. This meeting's importance was underscored by the fact that it brought together all department heads in the Memorial System with the President.

At that meeting, Mr. Warren stressed that this was to be a key theme of his administration. At one time, he noted, the idea of increasing employee productivity was seen as relevant only to the world of industry. Hospitals were looked upon only as service organizations where this element could not be measured and was not of real importance. Now, however, he noted, Memorial Hospital System has become a large, although nonprofit, corporation. It has its own sophisticated information systems which can be used to increase productivity, and to measure it, and it has its own department of Management Engineering. This department zeros in on the possibilities for developing Memorial's own leadership role in this new and vital area. With costs and public expectations rising simultaneously, improvement of hospital productivity can help keep costs down. "To address productivity," Mr. Warren said, "it is necessary to try and understand what it means. Productivity is not working harder. We're talking about working smarter, working in a more cost-productive manner, and upholding the quality of care we're proud of."

The vast program designed to equip all 3,500 Memorial employees for the productivity challenges of the 1980's will take more than a few months or a few years. But certain basic parts of it are in place already. The first series of programs, called "Issues for the Eighties—Managing Smarter," got underway early in 1980. This part of the program involved heads of departments throughout the System. In looking at the role of department heads in improving both productivity and the quality of work life, the emphasis was on positive input from the employees working together in small groups. As they discussed ways to "work smarter" with employees from other parts of the System, the department heads gained insight. They learned about general factors that have an impact on productivity, and also about specific aspects of their own managerial roles which could affect productivity.

This first stage, however, was only one part of what will be a massive educational program. There will also be an educational series tailored for supervisors, and then a series for other employees. The whole process involves employees from all segments of Memorial Hospital. An Assistant Vice President heads both a Productivity Steering Committee and an Educational Task Force. The Steering Committee addresses large general issues involved in productivity improvement; and the Educational Task Force will oversee the development and implementation of specific training programs related to the improving both of productivity and the quality of work life.

While the Memorial Hospital System in the 1980's has been looking inward for ways to improve productivity, it also has examined its own larger corporate structure. After a great deal of planning, and with the assistance of attorneys from the law firm of Fulbright and Jaworski, Memorial will enter into a massive reorganization of its legal and tax structure. The processes which make up this corporate restructuring are complex, and the results will certainly not be visible to the typical Memorial employee as he goes about his work. This reassignment of corporate assets and divisions, and the creation of holding companies will, however, enable Memorial to make better use of its nonprofit status in holding down health care costs.

Another new emphasis at Memorial Hospital System is its increased attempt to get outside the hospital to educate the community in ways which will affect the very basics of health care in the city. Mr. Warren talks about this aspect of Memorial's planning by explaining that "In the old days, people died from pneumonia, tuberculosis, and diarrhea." Today, we die from other causes—"from lifestyle problems: heart attacks, cancer, and accidents." Improvements in these areas will come only as we begin to change our lifestyles. The way to begin changing lifestyles is through education. Education has, of course, been a key part of Memorial since the days when Mrs. Jolly hired the first full-time nursing instructor, and Mr. Jolly spoke to the Houston newspapers on the need for hospital maternity care.

This new educational process, which involves an expansion of the School of Community Health Education, is somewhat different, however. What concerned the Jollys was education for medical personnel, and education of the American public to the availability and the advisability of quality hospital care. What Memorial, under Mr. Warren's leadership, now offers the people of Houston is education about ways to keep themselves healthy. The first of three courses offered in 1979 by Memorial's School of Community Health Education has now been greatly expanded. This year there are a large number of courses on such topics as weight control, prevention of heart disease, strokes, and cancer. There are also offerings in such other lifestyle-changing topics as coping with an aging parent and solving work-related problems. Now courses are offered at all three Houston hospitals, and last year 2,600 people from the Houston area attended such programs. The evidence mounts that this will be a continuing need for Houston and a very real way for Memorial to work toward disease prevention outside the walls of the hospital.

This expanding program of education handled through the School of Community Health Education is supplemented by Memorial's publications and media presentations. The hospital publishes a health newsletter called *For Your Good Health,* which reaches approximately 10,000 people each quarter with consumer-oriented health care information. Memorial also gives health care information to some 46,000 people annually who call in to its Health-Line. This service stocks more than 500 tapes on general health information ranging from nuclear medicine to nutrition.

THE KELLOG GRANT

Memorial's emphasis on staying healthy has been recognized by a $921,000 grant for the development and implementation of a three-year health promotion demonstration project. This grant, funded by the W. K. Kellog Foundation, is the largest such project they have funded in the state of Texas. The Kellog study will be supervised by Frank Webber, M.D., and by project director, John Sims. It will involve patients of the System's Family Practice Center located at Memorial Hospital, and also the 36 Family Practice Residents at Memorial.

The program seeks, explains Sims, "to take a healthy person, young or old, and keep him that way." "We do that by identifying potential health risks that a person has and doing something to reduce those risks." He goes on to explain that chronic diseases such as heart disease, cancer, and stroke cause more than 75 percent of all the deaths in the United States. Many of these could be prevented by simply reducing people's health risk factors. The Kellog Project at Memorial Hospital will focus on four of these risks: cigarette smoking, excessive stress, lack of exercise and being overweight. For the program, any patient with one of the four risks can be assigned to various ways to help him or her change such through physician counseling, educational programs, etc. Another group—the control group—will receive no such guidance during the evaluation period. At the end of six months and 12 months, all participants in the program will be checked to see if there have been significant changes in their lifestyle.

Memorial, as it looks both inside its own organization and outside into the community, also continues to develop in ways that will be familiar to those who have followed the history of the institution. One of these is through the acquisition of new, more highly specialized equipment. An example of this is the Department of Radiotherapy's recent purchase of a linear accelerator for radiation therapy. As Dr. DeWitt Cox, Director of the Radiology department said: "This is going to increase Memorial's range of treatment capabilities and brings us up-to-date in the state of the art technology in radiotherapy." The new machine can concentrate the radiation on the tumor without endangering nearby areas of the patient's body. It can also be used to penetrate deeper tumors than previous machines, and, because it works with a sophisticated computer that plans the course of radiation therapy for each patient, it can also determine with great precision exactly the right amount of radiation to administer.

With this sophisticated state of the art equipment, Memorial has also worked to bring about needed expansion of its Memorial Unit at Beechnut and the Southwest Freeway. This expansion will be Phase II of the original project which began in 1977; it will be a new 455-bed tower located adjacent to the original 600-bed hospital. Construction of the patient tower will begin in April 1984, with expected completion in July of 1986. The tower will cost $47 million to build, and another $15 million will be required to equip it. The Health Systems Agency of the Houston-Galveston Area Council has recommended the construction of the new tower to the Texas Health Facilities Commission, and the Commission is

Top Photo: Mr. and Mrs. Wilson Turner;
Bottom Photo: Retirement party for Mr.
Wilson Turner; Mrs. Turner is at left.

expected to give final approval of the tower by the end of the year.

The plans include educational facilities which will allow additional or expanded programs such as the Family Practice Residency Program, the School of Community Health Education, and several schools for nursing and allied health personnel. The auditorium of the new Quality of Life Building will be named the W. Wilson Turner Auditorium, in honor of the longtime President of the System.

In announcing the new program, Mr. William Warren, President of the Memorial Hospital System, made the following statement: "This second phase of development of the Memorial Unit has always been part of our long-range health care plans for Southwest Harris and East Fort Bend Counties. Our continuing high census pressures; the increasing regional demands for comprehensive health care services, and the ever-increasing requirements for education of health care personnel demonstrate the need for this project."

Because Mr. Warren's language is the language of today, it differs in tone from Reverend Pevoto's early lament that the hospital's biggest problem was "our prosperity in the matter of securing patients." The underlying pressure to expand has remained the same over the years, however, and it provides the continuity underneath the many changes and developments in the first 75 years of the Memorial Hospital System. Now, as in 1907, Memorial must keep expanding if it is to keep pace with the city it serves. Its many resources— dedicated and experienced leadership, a first-rate medical staff, a large number of employees dedicated both to the health-care profession and to the Memorial Hospital System, and its seventy-five-year record of service—will insure its continued success.

APPENDIX

Appendix A

MEMORIAL HOSPITAL SYSTEM

CHAIRMEN, BOARD OF TRUSTEES

1907 - 1915	Rev. J. L. Gross
1916 - 1919	R. E. Burt
1920 - 1938	Judge T. M. Kennerly
1939	J. W. Neal
1940	Walter H. Walne
1941 - 1945	J. E. Burkhart
1946 - 1948	A. D. Foreman
1949 - 1959	George M. Irving
1960 - 1964	Lester D. Cain
1965 - 1967	L. E. Frazier, Jr.
1968 - 1971	Vernon G. Garrett, Jr.
1972	Jackson C. Hinds
1973 -	Kenneth E. Montague

Appendix B

MEMORIAL HOSPITAL SYSTEM

CHIEF EXECUTIVE OFFICERS

1907 - 1917	Rev. D. R. Pevoto, Superintendent
1918 - 1920	Mrs. J. P. Burnett, Superintendent
1921 - 1936	Robert Jolly, Superintendent
1937 - 1945	Robert Jolly, Administrator
1946 (7 mos.)	A. D. Foreman, Acting Administrator
1946 - 1956	John G. Dudley, Administrator
1957 - 1962	John G. Dudley, Executive Director
1963 - 1970	W. Wilson Turner, Executive Director
1971 - 1980	W. Wilson Turner, President
1981 -	R. William Warren, President

Appendix C

MEMORIAL HOSPITAL SYSTEM

PRESIDENTS OF THE MEDICAL STAFF

1907	W. W. Ralston, M.D.	1945	Mark Latimer, M.D.
1908	W. W. Ralston, M.D.	1946	Abbe A. Ledbetter, M.D.
1909	E. M. Gray, M.D.	1947	J. G. Heard, M.D.
1910	J. B. York, M.D.	1948	Russell F. Bonham, M.D.
1911	S. J. Lister, M.D.	1949	John H. Wootters, M.D.
1912	E. G. Northrup, M.D.	1950	H. N. Gemoets, M.D.
1913	J. H. Foster, M.D.	1951	W. A. Sengelmann, M.D.
1914	E. L. Goar, M.D.	1952	Abe Hauser, M.D.
1915	M. B. Stokes, M.D.	1953	W. Frank Renfrow, M.D.
1916	J. B. York, M.D.	1954	Carlos R. Hamilton, M.D.
1917	Gavin Hamilton, M.D.	1955	J. Reese Blundell, M.D.
1918	S. M. Lister, M.D.	1956	F. Scott Glover, M.D.
1919	James A. Hill, M.D.	1957	Duncan C. McKeever, M.D.
1920	Judson L. Taylor M.D.	1958	Ed S. Crocker, M.D.
1921	A. E. Greer, M.D.	1959	Ronald F. Norris, M.D.
1922	B. W. Turner, M.D.	1960	Howard T. Barkley, M.D.
1923	E. Freeman Robbins, M.D.	1961	Ira S. Clarkson, M.D.
1924	E. M. Armstrong, M.D.	1962	Ed J. Morrow, M.D.
1925	T. H. Compere, M.D.	1963	Ben Walpole, M.D.
1926	W. E. Ramsay, M.D.	1964	A. T. Talley, Jr., M.D.
1927	W. W. Coulter, M.D.	1965	Homer A. Taylor, M.D.
1928	M. L. Brenner, M.D.	1966	A. W. Jester, M.D.
1929	M. J. Taylor, M.D.	1967	S. G. Ohlhausen, M.D.
1930	Paul V. Ledbetter, M.D.	1968	J. D. McCulley, M.D.
1931	P. R. Denman, M.D.	1969	Jack A. Haley, M.D.
1932	Ray K. Daily, M.D.	1970	Franz Leidler, M.D.
1933	G. H. Spurlock, M.D.	1971	E. M. Thomason, M.D.
1934	M. B. Stokes, M.D.	1972	D. W. Cox, Jr., M.D.
1935	Herman W. Johnson, M.D.	1973	William H. Kolter, M.D.
1936	A. T. Talley, M.D.	1974	Jack N. Bevil, M.D.
1937	J. H. Park, M.D.	1975	John E. Montgomery, M.D.
1938	L. E. Williford, M.D.	1976	Warren M. Scott, M.D.
1939	Herbert Hayes, M.D.	1977	Max C. Butler, M.D.
1940	C. M. Warner, M.D.	1978	Donald H. Nowlin, M.D.
1941	Frank Iiams, M.D.	1979	Lawrence W. Johnson, M.D.
1942	L. A. Myers, M.D.	1980	Bernard G. Vine, M.D.
1943	Dean H. Kendall, M.D.	1981	John R. Strawn, M.D.
1944	H. J. Ehlers, M.D.	1982	William L. Sheehan, M.D.

Appendix D

MEMORIAL HOSPITAL SYSTEM

CHIEFS OF STAFF

SOUTHWEST UNIT

1962	A. T. Talley, Jr., M.D.
1963	James R. Curbo, M.D.
1964	Tom P. Kennerly, M.D.
1965	Rhey H. Walker, II, M.D.
1966	Max C. Butler, M.D.
1967	C. E. Bancroft, M.D.
1968	William H. Kolter, M.D.
1969	William F. Ossenfort, M.D.
1970	C. Frank Webber, M.D.
1971	John R. Dunn, M.D.
1972	William C. Franklin, M.D.
1973	George O. Zenner, M.D.
1974	M. Derick Boldt, M.D.
1975	John R. Strawn, M.D.
1976	James M. Adkins, M.D.

SOUTHEAST UNIT

1964	B. A. Lawrence, M.D.
1965	L. W. Johnson, M.D.
1966	F. L. Phillips, M.D.
1967	J. W. Morrison, M.D.
1968	Harry E. Preble, M.D.
1969	I. M. Meisler, M.D.
1970	John E. Montgomery, M.D.
1971	J. D. Gerdes, M.D.
1972	R. G. McCorkle, M.D.
1973	Richard S. Mann, M.D.
1974	H. B. Woodward, M.D.
1975	C. W. Klanke, M.D.
1976	Charles H. Heider, M.D.
1977	W. L. Sheehan, M.D.
1978	R. E. Wilden, M.D.
1979	Price Campbell, M.D.

196

1980	Alan Baum, M.D.
1981	Hans Altinger, M.D.
1982	Robert Wallis, M.D.

CENTRAL UNIT

1969	Henry C. Maddox, III, M.D.
1970	John P. Stanford, M.D.
1971	Henry B. Holle, M.D.
1972	Bobbie Jones, M.D.
1973	P. O. Jones, M.D.
1974	Robert I. Cox, M.D.
1975	Wayne Viehweg, M.D.
1976	Donald H. Nowlin, M.D.

NORTHWEST UNIT

1966	E. Maurice Thomason, M.D.
1967	W. A. Grimes, M.D.
1968	Nelson W. Karbach, M.D.
1969	John W. Matthews, M.D.
1970	A. J. Haddock, M.D.
1971	W. H. Spankus, M.D.
1972	J. W. Baxter, M.D.
1973	Warren M. Scott, M.D.
1974	F. M. Rembert, M.D.
1975	V. C. Mascio, M.D.
1976	E. Maurice Thomason, M.D.
1977	B. G. Vine, M.D.
1978	A. E. Smith, M.D.
1979	G. W. Maness, M.D.
1980	J. B. Tang, M.D.
1981	John J. Milligan, M.D.
1982	James A. Smelley, M.D.

MEMORIAL HOSPITAL

1977	Henry B. Holle, M.D.
1978	Robert I. Cox, M.D.
1979	Charles Stephenson, M.D.
1980	Winnie Crump, M.D.
1981	Robert I. Hauser, M.D.
1982	Jim F. Waldron, M.D.

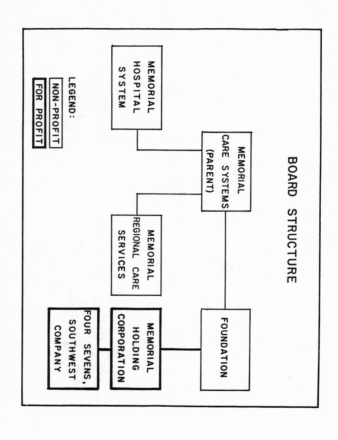

BOARD STRUCTURE

MEMORIAL
HOSPITAL
SYSTEM

MEMORIAL
CARE SYSTEMS
(PARENT)

MEMORIAL
REGIONAL CARE
SERVICES

FOUNDATION

MEMORIAL
HOLDING
CORPORATION

FOUR SEVENS,
SOUTHWEST
COMPANY

LEGEND:
NON-PROFIT
FOR PROFIT

Appendix E

Appendix F

MEMORIAL CARE SYSTEMS

BOARD OF TRUSTEES

1982

B. J. Bradshaw
William W. Bryan
Dr. Kenneth L. Chafin
Paul R. Cole
Mary Frances Couper (Mrs. Fred)
Dr. Milton E. Cunningham
Lanson B. Ditto
Jerry E. Finger
L. E. Frazier, Jr.
Vernon G. Garrett, Jr.
F. O'Neil Griffin
John G. Heard
Jackson C. Hinds
Melvin E. Kurth, Jr.
Paul E. Martin
Kline McGee
Kenneth E. Montague
S. I. Morris
Harry W. Patterson
Dr. James S. Riley
Judson W. Robinson, Jr.
Orrien R. Smith
Robert Stewart, Jr.
M. Turhan Taner
W. Wilson Turner
R. William Warren
Bernard Weingarten
Loise Wessendorff (Mrs. Joseph)
Robert E. Wise

CORPORATE OFFICERS

Chairman	K. E. Montague
Vice Chairman	John G. Heard
Vice Chairman	B. J. Bradshaw
President	R. William Warren
Vice President	Joe Lamendola
Vice President	Richard D. Branum
Vice President	Warren Wishnack
Vice President	Robert B. Stevenson
Vice President	R. Eugene Ross
Secretary	Maxine Calhoun
Treasurer	Bob Dyer
Controller	Simon Scholtz

Appendix G

MEMORIAL CARE SYSTEMS

COMMITTEES

1982

EXECUTIVE
>Kenneth E. Montague, Chairman
>W. Wilson Turner
>William W. Bryan
>L. E. Frazier, Jr.
>Bernard Weingarten
>Jackson C. Hinds
>Paul R. Cole
>Vernon G. Garrett, Jr.
>R. William Warren
>John G. Heard
>B. J. Bradshaw

FINANCE AND BUDGET
>Paul R. Cole, Chairman
>Bill Barnard
>Bernard Weingarten
>Vernon G. Garrett, Jr.
>F. O'Neil Griffin

PERSONNEL
>Kline McGee, Chairman
>Harry W. Patterson
>Lanson B. Ditto
>O. R. Smith
>Bernard Weingarten

INSURANCE

William W. Bryan, Chairman
L. E. Frazier, Jr.
Robert E. Wise
Judson W. Robinson, Jr.
W. Wilson Turner

AUDIT

Robert E. Wise, Chairman
Robert Stewart
Paul E. Martin, Jr.
Vernon G. Garrett, Jr.
Melvin E. Kurth, Jr.

Appendix H

MEMORIAL HOSPITAL FOUNDATION OF HOUSTON

PRESIDENTS

1971	Vernon G. Garrett, Jr.
1972 -	Kline McGee

DIRECTORS

1982

Lanson B. Ditto
S. I. Morris
Kline McGee
Robert E. Wise
Jackson C. Hinds
Paul E. Martin

OFFICERS

Kline McGee, President
Robert E. Wise, Vice President
Lanson B. Ditto, Secretary-Treasurer

Appendix I

MEMORIAL REGIONAL CARE SERVICES

BOARD OF TRUSTEES

1982

Paul R. Cole, Chairman

S. I. Morris

F. O'Neil Griffin

John G. Heard

Vernon G. Garrett, Jr.

Dr. Kenneth L. Chafin

Bill Barnard

CORPORATE OFFICERS

President	R. William Warren
Vice President	Bob Shaw
Treasurer	Bob G. Dyer
Secretary	Maxine Calhoun

Appendix J

MEMORIAL HOLDING CORPORATION

BOARD OF TRUSTEES

1982

Vernon G. Garrett, Jr., Chairman

L. E. Frazier, Jr.

Melvin E. Kurth, Jr.

Robert Stewart, Jr.

Paul R. Cole

CORPORATE OFFICERS

President	R. William Warren
Vice President	James P. Miller
Treasurer	Bob G. Dyer
Secretary	Maxine Calhoun

Appendix K

FOUR SEVENS, SOUTHWEST COMPANY

BOARD OF TRUSTEES

1982

Vernon G. Garrett, Jr., Chairman

L. E. Frazier, Jr.

Melvin E. Kurth, Jr.

Robert Stewart, Jr.

Paul R. Cole

CORPORATE OFFICERS

President	R. William Warren
Vice President	James P. Miller
Treasurer	Bob G. Dyer
Secretary	Maxine Calhoun

Appendix L

MEMORIAL HOSPITAL SYSTEM, HOUSTON, TEXAS

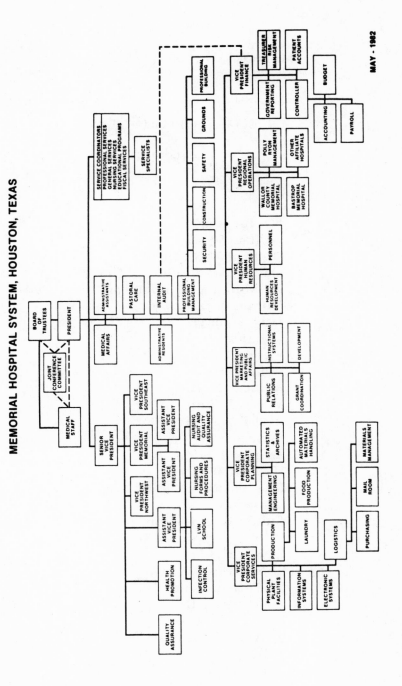

MAY - 1982

Appendix M

MEMORIAL HOSPITAL SYSTEM

BOARD OF TRUSTEES

1982

B.J. Bradshaw
William W. Bryan
Dr. Kenneth L. Chafin
Mary Frances Couper (Mrs. Fred)
Dr. Milton E. Cunningham
Lanson B. Ditto
Jerry E. Finger
L. E. Frazier, Jr.
Vernon G. Garrett, Jr.
John G. Heard
Jackson C. Hinds
Melvin E. Kurth
Paul E. Martin
Kline McGee
Kenneth E. Montague
Harry W. Patterson
Blye Philpott (Mrs. E. W.)
Dr. James S. Riley
Judson W. Robinson, Jr.
Warren M. Scott, M.D.
Orrien R. Smith
Robert Stewart, Jr.
M. Turhan Taner
W. Wilson Turner
R. William Warren
Bernard Weingarten
Loise Wessendorff (Mrs. Joseph)
Robert E. Wise

Appendix N

MEMORIAL HOSPITAL SYSTEM

COMMITTEES

1982

EXECUTIVE
Kenneth E. Montague, Chairman
William W. Bryan
B. J. Bradshaw
L. E. Frazier, Jr.
Jackson C. Hinds
John G. Heard
Paul R. Cole
Vernon G. Garrett, Jr.

FINANCE & BUDGET
Paul R. Cole, Chairman
Kline McGee
Warren M. Scott, M.D.
W. Wilson Turner
Bernard Weingarten

AUDIT
Robert E. Wise, Chairman
Robert Stewart
Paul E. Martin
Vernon G. Garrett, Jr.
Melvin E. Kurth

PERSONNEL
Kline McGee, Chairman
Harry W. Patterson
Lanson B. Ditto
Orrien R. Smith
Bernard Weingarten

BYLAWS
John G. Heard, Chairman
B. J. Bradshaw
L. E. Frazier, Jr.

NOMINATING
Vernon G. Garrett, Jr.
Jackson C. Hinds
L. E. Frazier, Jr.

H.B.U. LIAISON
B. J. Bradshaw, Chairman
L. E. Frazier, Jr.
Vernon G. Garrett, Jr.

PASTORAL CARE
Milton Cunningham, Chairman
Kenneth L. Chafin
James S. Riley
James Ray Roach
LeRay Fowler
Andy Davis

EDUCATION
Jerry E. Finger, Chairman
M. Turhan Taner
Kenneth L. Chafin
Blye Philpott
Mary Frances Couper
S. I. Morris

INSURANCE
William W. Bryan, Chairman
L. E. Frazier, Jr.
Robert E. Wise
Judson W. Robinson, Jr.
W. Wilson Turner

PLANNING & DEVELOPMENT
Jackson C. Hinds, Chairman
Kenneth E. Montague
Warren M. Scott, M.D.
John G. Heard
Robert Stewart, Jr.
Paul R. Cole
Vernon G. Garrett, Jr.
Loise Wessendorff
W. Wilson Turner
Melvin E. Kurth, Jr.
William Sheehan, M.D.
Jim Waldron, M.D.
James A. Smelley, M.D.
Robert Wallis, M.D.

JOINT CONFERENCE
Kenneth E. Montague
L. E. Frazier, Jr.
Warren M. Scott, M.D.
B. J. Bradshaw
Kenneth L. Chafin
John G. Heard
R. William Warren
Jerry Brooks
John R. Strawn, M.D.
William Sheehan, M.D.
V. C. Mascio, M.D.
Jim Waldron, M.D.
James Smelley, M.D.
Robert Wallis, M.D.

AD HOC BLDG. COM. AMB. CARE CENTER
Orrien R. Smith, Chairman
William W. Bryan
Bernard Weingarten
Warren M. Scott, M.D.
W. Wilson Turner

Appendix O

MEMORIAL HOSPITAL SYSTEM

CORPORATE OFFICERS

1982

Chairman of the Board	Kenneth E. Montague
Vice Chairman	B. J. Bradshaw
Vice Chairman	John G. Heard
President	R. William Warren
Senior Vice President	Jerry Brooks
Vice President, Finance	Warren Wishnack
Vice President, Marketing and Public Affairs	Robert B. Stevenson
Vice President, Corporate Planning	Richard D. Branum
Vice President, Corporate Services	Joe Lamendola
Vice President, Human Resources	Eugene Ross
Vice President, Regional Operations	Bob Shaw
Vice President	Michael F. O'Keefe
Vice President	Ken Wine
Vice President	Steve Sanders
Assistant Vice President	Walter Wilson
Assistant Vice President	Donna Denny
Assistant Vice President	Opal Bevil
Assistant Vice President	Fay Peyton
Secretary	Maxine Calhoun
Treasurer	Bob G. Dyer
Controller	Simon Scholtz
Assistant Secretary	Richard D. Branum

Appendix P

SYSTEM:

President .... William L. Sheehan, M.D.
President-elect .... Valenzio C. Mascio, M.D.
Vice President .... Henry B. Holle, M.D.
Secretary .... Alan C. Baum, M.D.

UNITS:

MEMORIAL

Chief of Staff .... Jim F. Waldron, M.D.
Chief of Staff-elect .... Ernest Max, M.D.
Vice Chief of Staff .... Robert F. Ezell, M.D.
Secretary .... George E. Whalen, M.D.

NORTHWEST

Chief of Staff .... James A. Smelley, M.D.
Chief of Staff-elect .... Edward E. Kearns, M.D.
Vice Chief of Staff .... Beryl L. Harberg, M.D.
Secretary .... A. J. Haddock, M.D.

SOUTHEAST

Chief of Staff .... Robert Wallis, M.D.
Chief of Staff-elect .... Moises Lopez, M.D.
Vice Chief of Staff .... Chris Cabler, M.D.
Secretary .... Volker Eisele, M.D.

SYSTEM DEPARTMENT CHIEFS

Anesthesiology .... Richard C. Hay, M.D.
General Practice .... Lawrence W. Johnson, M.D.
Medicine .... John E. Montgomery, M.D.
Neuro-Psychiatry .... Cal K. Cohn, M.D.
Obstetrics & Gynecology ...... Valenzio Mascio, M.D.
Pathology .... Zack R. Blailock, M.D.
Pediatrics .... Raymond H. Mondshine, M.D.
Radiology .... Donald J. Sumerlin, M.D.
Surgery .... Henry B. Holle, M.D.

Appendix Q

1982

SERVICE AND SECTION CHAIRMEN

MEMORIAL HOSPITAL SYSTEM MEDICAL STAFF

SYSTEM

Pathology Service	Zack Blailock, M.D.
Radiology Service	Donald Sumerlin, M.D.

MEMORIAL

Anesthesiology Service	Richard Hay, M.D.
General Practice Service	Charles Neilson, M.D.
Family Practice Section	Charles Neilson, M.D.
Medicine Service	Samuel Boushy, M.D.
Dermatology Section	Norman Guzick, M.D.
Internal Medicine Section	Samuel Boushy, M.D.
Neuro-Psychiatry Service	Cal Cohn, M.D.
Neurology Section	William Fleming, M.D.
Psychiatry Section	Cal Cohn, M.D.
Ob/Gyn Service	Jon Knolle, M.D.
Pediatric Service	Raymond Mondshine, M.D.
Surgery Service	Henry Holle, M.D.
General Dentistry Section	Thomas Janson, M.D.
General Surgery Section	N. Perryman Colling, M.D., Chairman
	Michael Gallagher, M.D. Vice Chairman
Neurosurgery Section	Frank Yelin, M.D.
Ophthalmology Section	Stephen White, M.D.
Oral & Maxillofacial Surgery Section	James V. Johnson, D.D.S.
Otorhinolaryngology & Head & Neck Surgery Section	George Card, M.D.
Orthopaedic Section	W. Lin Jones, M.D.
Urology Section	Robert I. Cox, M.D.

SOUTHEAST

General Practice Service	L. W. Johnson, M.D.
Medicine Service	John Montgomery, M.D.
Ob/Gyn Service	Richard Mann, M.D.
Ophthalmology Section	Richard Pitts, M.D.
Orthopedic Section	Booker Wright, M.D.

214

Pediatric Service	Jovita Falgout, M.D.
Surgery Service	Price Campbell, M.D.

NORTHWEST

Anesthesia Service...............	Rady Villaflor, M.D.
General Practice Service	Gerald Maness, M.D.
General Surgery Section	Alfred E. Smith, M.D.
Medicine Service	Victor Vlahakas, M.D.
Ob/Gyn Service	Valenzio Mascio, M.D.
Ophthalmology Section	Michael Spiegelman, M.D.
Orthopaedic Section.............	Arthur Mendelow, M.D.
Pediatric Service	W. S. Smith, M.D.
Surgery Service	Robert Whitsell, M.D.
Urology Section	Eugene Goldman, M.D.

Appendix R

216

TISSUE
Henry B. Holle, M.D., Chairman
V. C. Mascio, M.D.
Lawrence Johnson, M.D.
James Lawhon, M.D.
Bob E. Stout, M.D.
Charles Pehr, M.D.
Jose B. Tang, Jr., M.D.
Po-Wen Lee, M.D.
Luis G. Valdes, M.D.
Alfred Smith, M.D.
John J. Milligan, M.D.

CREDENTIALS & MEDICAL ETHICS
Christopher Kaeppel, M.D.
Mark Lambert, M.D.
Burton Silverman, M.D.
Raymond Witt, M.D.
Samuel Boushy, M.D.
Bob Stout, M.D.
Harold Miller, M.D.
Chris Angelo, D.O.
Cal Cohn, M.D.
W. H. Spankus, M.D.
M. J. Gould, M.D.
J. B. Tang, Jr., M.D.
Richard McLaughlin, M.D.
A. J. Haddock, M.D.
Ford Cashion, M.D.
Valenzio C. Mascio, M.D.
Alfred E. Smith, M.D.
Warren Scott, M.D.
Manuel Munoz, M.D.
Joe Atlas, M.D.
Irwin Meisler, M.D.
Harris Rotman, M.D.
Louis Valdes, M.D.
Michael Hunter, D.O.
Steven Goldstein, M.D.
Stanley Pool, M.D.
Horacio Guzman, M.D.

Appendix S

MEMORIAL HOSPITAL SYSTEM
1982 UNIT MEDICAL STAFF COMMITTEES
MEMORIAL HOSPITAL

CRITICAL CARE COMMITTEE

Ronald Mahoney, M.D., Chairman
Paul Garcia, M.D.
Charles Crumb, M.D.
Bob Stout, M.D.
Martin Steiner, M.D.
William Hensel, M.D.

INFECTION CONTROL COMMITTEE

Edward Septimus, M.D., Chairman
Harold Pruessner, M.D.
Chris Kaeppel, M.D.
Luis Mateo, M.D.
Joan Stoerner, M.D.
W. Lin Jones, M.D.
Glen Lewis, M.D.

AMBULATORY CARE AND DISASTER COMMITTEE

Louis Neff, M.D., Chairman
David Prentice, M.D.
Hugh Gilmore, M.D.
William Kolter, M.D.
O. Gaynor Janes, M.D.
Robert E. Davis, M.D.
David Cotlar, M.D.
Luis Mateo, M.D.

DeWitt Cox, M.D.
Paul Brindley, M.D.
Joan Nish, M.D.
Cal Cohn, M.D.

MEDICAL CARE EVALUATION COMMITTEE

William Franklin, M.D., Chairman
Edward Blackburn, M.D.
Don Baxter, M.D.
Robert Conte, M.D.
Thomas J. Lawhon, M.D.
Sharon Lewis, M.D.
William St. Clair, M.D.
David Peterson, M.D.

OPERATING ROOM COMMITTEE

Richard Hay, M.D., Chairman
Jon Knolle, M.D.
Thomas Janson, D.D.S.
N. Perryman Collins, M.D.
Frank Yelin, M.D.
Stephen White, M.D.
James V. Johnson, D.D.S.
W. Lin Jones, M.D.
George Card, M.D.
Robert Cox, M.D.
Homer Taylor, M.D.
Robert Wildin, M.D.

DELIVERY ROOM COMMITTEE

Jon Knolle, M.D., Chairman
Robert Mardock, M.D.
Robert Viles, M.D.
Charles Bancroft, M.D.
Nancy Dickey, M.D.
Joan Stoerner, M.D.

PHARMACY, THERAPEUTICS AND I.V. THERAPY COMMITTEE

Robert Barr, M.D., Chairman
Edward Septimus, M.D.
George Zenner, M.D.
Charles Conant, M.D.
Raymond Witt, M.D.
Burton Silverman, M.D.

Appendix T

MEMORIAL HOSPITAL SYSTEM
1982 UNIT MEDICAL STAFF COMMITTEES
SOUTHEAST HOSPITAL

EXECUTIVE COMMITTEE

Robert Wallis, M.D., Chairman
Moises Lopez, M.D.
Chris Cabler, M.D.
Hans Altinger, M.D.
Jovita Falgout, M.D.
L. W. Johnson, M.D.
John Montgomery, M.D.
Booker Wright, M.D.
Michael Hunter, M.D.
Richard Pitts, M.D.
Price Campbell, M.D.
Volker Eisele, M.D.

AMBULATORY CARE AND DISASTER COMMITTEE

Luis Valdes, M.D., Chairman
David Prentice, M.D.
M. Alloju, M.D.
Manuel Bustos, M.D.
Richard Mann, M.D.
Ursula Fraustadt, M.D.
Felipe Rios, M.D.
Luis Mateo, M.D.
Richard Bryan, M.D.
Volker Eisele, M.D.

MEDICAL CARE EVALUATION COMMITTEE

Hans Altinger, M.D., Chairman
Carol Lopas, M.D.
Horacio Guzman, M.D.
Richard Materson, M.D.
Irwin Meisler, M.D.
Ursula Fraustadt, M.D.
Chris Cabler, M.D.;
Luis Mateo, M.D.

PHARMACY, THERAPEUTICS AND I.V. THERAPY COMMITTEE

Charlea Heider, M.D., Chairman
Manuel Bustos, M.D.
Stanley Pool, M.D.
Laurie Brown, M.D.
O. Fernandez, M.D.

DELIVERY ROOM COMMITTEE

Michael Hunter, D.O., Chairman
Jovita Falgout, M.D.
Charles Lobb, M.D.
Volker Eisele, M.D.

INFECTION CONTROL COMMITTEE

Edward George, M.D., Chairman
Anthony O'Dwyer, M.D.
Charles Lobb, M.D.
B. A. Lawrence, M.D.
Rathna Sastry, M.D.
Mark Gilden, M.D.
Luis Mateo, M.D.

NURSING ADVISORY COMMITTEE

Chris Cabler, M.D., Chairman
P. W. Lee, M.D.
Brian Schulman, M.D.
Kenneth Straw, M.D.
Arun Mukhopadhyay, M.D.

OPERATING ROOM COMMITTEE

Price Campbell, M.D., Chairman
Elihut Ravelo, M.D.
Booker Wright, M.D.
Richard Pitts, M.D.
Michael Hunter, D.O.
Horacio Guzman, M.D.
Sherwin Kershman, D.D.S.
Volker Eisele, M.D.

CRITICAL CARE COMMITTEE

John Montgomery, M.D., Chairman
Brian Schulman, M.D.
L. W. Johnson, M.D.
Luis Valdes, M.D.
Volker Eisele, M.D.
M. Alloju, M.D.

NOMINATING COMMITTEE

John Montgomery, M.D., Chairman
L. W. Johnson, M.D.
Chris Cabler, M.D.
Richard Mann, M.D.
Luis Valdes, M.D.

Appendix U

MEMORIAL HOSPITAL SYSTEM
1982 UNIT MEDICAL STAFF COMMITTEES
NORTHWEST HOSPITAL

EXECUTIVE COMMITTEE

James A. Smelley, M.D.,
     Chairman
Edward E. Kearns, M.D.
Beryl L. Harberg, M.D.
Andy J. Haddock, M.D.
John Milligan, M.D.
Rady Villaflor, M.D.
Gerald W. Maness, M.D.
Victor Vlahakos, M.D.
Valenzio Mascio, M.D.
William S. Smith, M.D.
Abraham Mendelow, M.D.
Eugene Goldman, M.D.
Alfred E. Smith, M.D.
Michael Spiegelman, M.D.

EX-OFFICIO MEMBERS

Willson J. Fahlberg, Ph. D.
Frank M. Rembert, M.D.
Jose B. Tang, Jr., M.D.
Carl Rountree, M.D.

NOMINATING COMMITTEE

Walter L. Prater, D.D.S.,
     Chairman
John J. Milligan, M.D.

Jose B. Tang, Jr., M.D.
Gerald W. Maness, M.D.
Warren M. Scott, M.D.

DELIVERY ROOM COMMITTEE

Valenzio Mascio, M.D.,
    Chairman
Ming C. Hsu, M.D.
Melchor M. Boone, M.D.

AMBULATORY CARE AND DISASTER

Jose B. Tang, Jr., M.D.,
    Chairman
James A. Butler, M.D.
Edgar M. Thomason, M.D.
Kenneth Korsah, M.D.
Michael L. Wexler, M.D.
E. Wiley Biles, M.D.

INFECTION CONTROL COMMITTEE

Herman Reyes, D.O., Chairman
Kanubhai P. Mehta, M.D.
So-Kim Tan Chiu, M.D.
Heena N. Thakkar, M.D.
Bernard G. Vine, M.D.

OPERATING ROOM COMMITTEE

Eugene Goldman, M.D.,
    Chairman
Abraham L. Mendelow, M.D.
Alfred E. Smith, M.D.
Michael Spiegelman, M.D.
Valenzio Mascio, M.D.
Rady Villaflor, M.D.
Edward Kearns, M.D.

PHARMACY, THERAPEUTIC AND I.V. THERAPY COMMITTEE

Hubert L. Smith, M.D., Chairman
Kanubhai P. Mehta, M.D.
Michael N. Goldberg, M.D.
John William Matthews, M.D.
Bernard H. Feldman, M.D.

NURSING SERVICE ADVISORY COMMITTEE

Wilford A. Grimes, M.D., Chairman
Tara H. Shani, M.D.
Harold S. Joachim, M.D.
Thomas N. Corpening, M.D.
Peter S. Dawson, M.D.
Abdul G. Memon, M.D.
William V. Cruce, M.D.
Joseph S. Montgomery, M.D.

MEDICAL CARE EVALUATION COMMITTEE

Carl B. Rountree, M.D., Chairman
Edgar M. Thomason, M.D.
Willerd Spankus, M.D.
Warren M. Scott, Jr., M.D.
Michael L. Wexler, M.D.
John P. Stanford, Jr., M.D.
Alfred E. Smith, M.D.

CRITICAL CARE COMMITTEE

Kanuehai P. Mehta, M.D., Chairman
Willerd H. Spankus, M.D.
Warren M. Scott, Jr., M.D.
Zayd Kaylani, M.D.
Beryl Harberg, M.D.
Gerald W. Maness, M.D.

Appendix V

MEMORIAL HOSPITAL SYSTEM

BED CAPACITY

1982

Unit	Beds Licensed	Open
Southeast	235	215
Northwest	230	218
Memorial	600	565
Sub Total	1,065	998

AFFILIATED HOSPITALS

Memorial Hospital of Waller County Hempstead, Texas	34	31
Bastrop Memorial Hospital Bastrop, Texas	25	25
Sub Total	59	56

MANAGED HOSPITALS

Polly Ryon Memorial Hospital Richmond, Texas	99	99
Total	1,223	1,153

Appendix W

MEMORIAL HOSPITAL SYSTEM
AFFILIATED EDUCATION PROGRAM

PROGRAM	AFFILIATION
Administrative Residency Program	George Washington University Trinity University
Blood Bank Technology	University of Texas Health Science Center at Houston
Dietetic Internship	Texas Woman's University
Emergency Medical Technicians (Advanced)	University of Texas Health Science Center at Houston
Emergency Medical Technicians (Basic)	Houston Community College San Jacinto Junior College Manville Volunteer Pearland — Programs
Engineering Program	Texas A&M University —College of Engineering
ENT Residency Program	University of Texas Medical Branch at Galveston
Family Practice Residency	University of Texas Medical School at Houston
Junior Clerkship for Medical Students	University of Texas Medical School at Houston

Medical Education Community Orientation	American Student Medical Association
Medical Technology, School of	Houston Baptist University Lamar University Sam Houston State University University of Texas at Austin
Occupational Therapy	Houston Community College Texas Woman's University University of Florida University of North Dakota University of Texas Medical Branch at Galveston University of Texas Medical School at San Antonio
Operating Room Technicians Program	Houston Community College
Pharmacy Intern Program	University of Houston University of Texas Texas Southern University
Physical Therapy Program	Texas Woman's University
Registered Medical Records Administration	Southwest Texas State University University of Southwestern Louisiana University of Texas at Galveston
Registered Nurses Program	Houston Baptist University Houston Community College Texas Woman's University, Institute of Health Science

229

(Registered Nurses Program, continued)	University of Texas Health Science Center at Houston Wharton County Junior College District
Social Services (Graduate)	University of Houston University of Iowa
Social Services (Undergraduate)	Houston Baptist University Sam Houston University
Speech Pathology	University of Houston
Vocational Nursing Program	Houston Community College

MEMORIAL HOSPITAL SYSTEM
EDUCATION PROGRAMS

PROGRAM	COORDINATORS
Community Health Education, School	Charles Berry, M.D.
Health Line	Charles Berry, M.D.
Hospital Chaplaincy Program	Tom Cole
Medical Technology, School of	Kathy Mathy, MT, (ASCP), MS
Pharmacy Extern Program	Harland Henry, R. Ph.
Radiologic Technology, School of	Rita Cusworth
Registered Nurse Internship	Beverly Brewer, RN
Registered Nurse Refresher Course	Beverly Brewer, RN
Vocational Nursing School	Fay Peyton, RN

INDEX